FOR ORGANS, PIANOS, ELECTRONIC AND DIGITAL INSTRUMENTS

E•Z PLAY TODAY

302

More Kid's Songfest
AN EASY BOOK OF MUSICAL FUN FOR CHILDREN!

Musical Things to Learn

The Music Alphabet 2
The Staff 2
Playing Your Keyboard 3
How to Read EZ Play Notation 4
Counting Beats and Rhythms 4
Bar Lines and Time Signatures 5
Sharps, Flats, and Naturals 6
More Musical Signs and Symbols 6

Activity Pages to Have Fun With

Musical Words 14
Crossword Fun 24
Connect the Dots 33
Word Search 43
Note Reading Review 53
Music Math 62
Find the Hidden Objects 63
Maze Fun 72
Music Matching 82
Answer Key 88

Songs to Play

ABC 8
All My Loving 10
The Ballad of Davy Crockett 9
The Bare Necessities 12
Brown Eyed Girl 16
Candle on the Water 18

Casper the Friendly Ghost 20
Count Your Blessings Instead of Sheep 22
Do-Re-Mi 28
Don't Be Cruel (To a Heart That's True) 25
Everything Is Beautiful 30
Gonna Build a Mountain 34
Happy Birthday to You 36
Happy Trails 38
The Hokey Pokey 37
I'm a Believer 40
I'd Like to Teach the World to Sing 44
If I Had a Hammer 48
Lean on Me 50
Let the Sunshine In 47
Linus and Lucy 54
The Marvelous Toy 56
Me and You and a Dog Named Boo 58
The Medallion Calls 60
On the Good Ship Lollipop 64
Peter Cottontail 66
The Rainbow Connection 68
Stand by Me 70
Sugar, Sugar 73
Surfin' Safari 76
Winnie the Pooh 78
This Land Is Your Land 81
Won't You Be My Neighbor? 83
Yellow Submarine 86

ISBN 978-1-4768-7564-4

T0039554

HAL•LEONARD®
CORPORATION

7777 W. BLUEMOUND RD. P.O. BOX 13819 MILWAUKEE, WI 53213

The **ABCs of**

FOR ORGANS, PIANOS & ELECTRONIC KEYBOARDS

Playing Music is Fun and Easy!

THE MUSIC ALPHABET

The English language has 26 letters in its alphabet. The **music alphabet** uses only the first seven letters: A, B, C, D, E, F, G.

THE STAFF

Music is written on a **staff** of five lines and four spaces. A **clef sign** designates which notes the lines and spaces represent. Each line and space has a letter name; one of the letters of the music alphabet. The higher on the staff a note is written, the higher the note will sound. This book uses notes written on the **treble** staff.

Here are some tricks to help you remember the names of the notes on the treble staff.

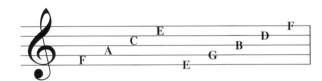

To remember the notes written in the **spaces**, notice that the letters, from bottom to top, spell the word **"FACE."** Just think, "There's a **FACE** in the space."

To remember the notes written on the **lines**, think, "Every Good Boy Does Fine." From bottom to top, the first letter of each word in that sentence matches the letter names of the lines.

Each key on the keyboard has a letter name from the music alphabet. Since there are only seven letters, they're repeated over and over. A note can have the same letter name but sound higher or lower. This is called **pitch**. For example, a C in the middle of the keyboard and the C eight notes above have the same name, but the middle C sounds lower. When reading the note names be sure to note how high or low the note is written on the staff, so you can play the note on the correct place on the keyboard.

PLAYING YOUR KEYBOARD

Accompaniment Keys

The keys on the left side of your keyboard will play the accompaniment notes. Use your left hand to play these notes. Apply the UNCOLORED stickers on these keys as shown in the picture.

Melody Keys

The melody keys start on Middle C and move to the right. Use your right hand to play these keys. Apply the colored stickers to these keys as shown in the picture.

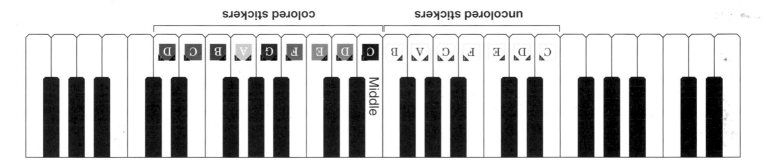

Middle C is a reference point found in most of the songs in this book. Once you've found Middle C, you'll know you're playing the melody in the correct place. Locating Middle C depends on the kind of keyboard you have.

Acoustic Pianos: To find Middle C, look for the brand name, usually in the middle of the piano directly above the keys. The C just below the brand name is Middle C, right in the middle of the keyboard.

Electronic Keyboards and Digital Pianos: Generally Middle C is the first C to the right of the chord keys. Many electronic keyboards are different. The best way to identify your chord keys and Middle C is to consult your owner's manual.

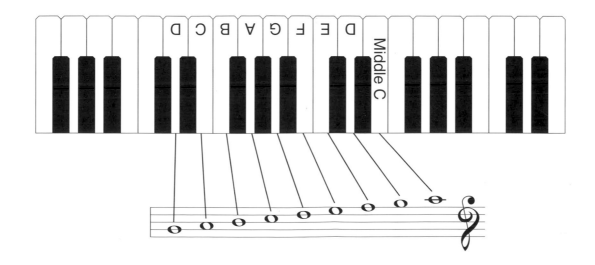

HOW TO READ EZ PLAY NOTATION

Color Coding

Each melody note has a specific color. To play each song, match the color on the music (under each note on the staff) with the color of the keyboard sticker. Each note is also named by letter. If you know the letter names of the keys you can also read the music in this way.

Optional Harmony or Chord Accompaniment

The uncolored stickers can be applied below Middle C if you wish. You can use your left hand to play harmony or an accompaniment by playing the note named in the box above the melody. Hold down the left-hand note indicated until another letter appears. If your keyboard has chord accompaniment keys or buttons, you can use these in the same way.

Instrument Settings

An instrument setting is indicated for each song. This is just a suggestion and ANY instrument setting can be used. Be creative!

Rhythm Settings

A rhythm setting is indicated for each song. If a song has a 3 at the beginning, use the Waltz setting. However, if there is a 4 at the beginning, ROCK, SWING, or any other rhythm can be used, even if only one rhythm is suggested.

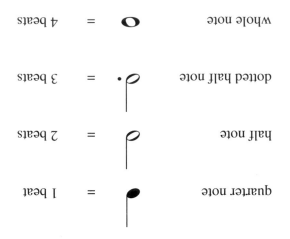

↑ Waltz setting

↑ Rock, Swing or other rhythm

COUNTING BEATS AND RHYTHMS

All songs use different types of **notes** to represent long and short sounds. Each note relates to **the beat**, the steady rhythmic pulse of the music.

quarter note	♩	=	1 beat
half note	♩	=	2 beats
dotted half note	♩.	=	3 beats
whole note	𝅝	=	4 beats

The quarter note can be divided.

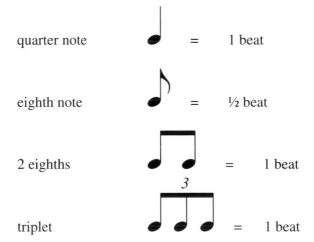

Rests are used to indicate silence, or when not to play. There is a rest to match each note value.

quarter rest	ζ	=	1 beat
half rest	▬	=	2 beats
whole rest	▬	=	4 beats (or whole measure)
eighth rest	⁊	=	½ beat

BAR LINES AND TIME SIGNATURES

To make reading easier, the staff is divided by **bar lines** into equal segments called **measures**.
A **double bar** is placed at the end of the song.

A **time signature** is placed at the beginning of every song. The top number of the time signature tells you how many beats are in each measure. So, for example, if the top number is 4, there are 4 beats in every measure.

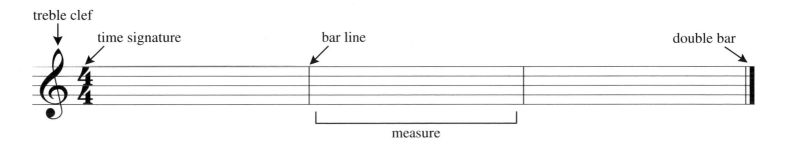

SHARPS, FLATS, AND NATURALS

A **sharp** sign ♯ raises the pitch of a note a half-step. On the keyboard, a sharp is usually played on a black key.

For example, C♯ is the black key between C and D. F♯ is the black key between F and G.

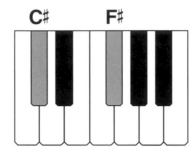

A **flat** sign ♭ lowers a pitch a half-step. Flats are usually played on the black keys. On the keyboard, B♭ is the black key between B and A. E♭ is between E and D.

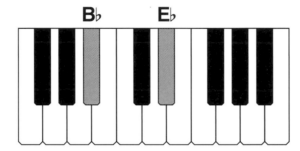

Sharps and flats stay sharp or flat for an entire measure, unless you see a **natural** sign: ♮

The natural sign **cancels** a sharp or flat.

MORE MUSICAL SIGNS AND SYMBOLS
Ties

A curved line connecting two notes with the same pitch is called a **tie**.

It "ties" the two notes together. The first note is played and counted for its full value, plus the value of the note it's tied to. The tied note is not played again. That's why there's not a letter inside the second note. A tie gives the note a longer value.

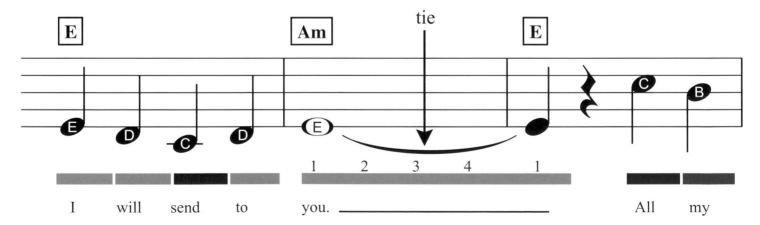

Repeat Sign

A **repeat sign** directs you to repeat a song, or part of a song. When you come to the two dots of the sign, go back and play that portion of the music again.

1st and 2nd Ending

In addition to a repeat sign, sometimes a **1st and 2nd ending sign** will be used. Play the repeated section as indicated, but instead of repeating the measure marked with the 1st ending, skip ahead to the measure marked 2nd ending, continuing on to the end of the song. This sign is often used when there is more than one verse in a song.

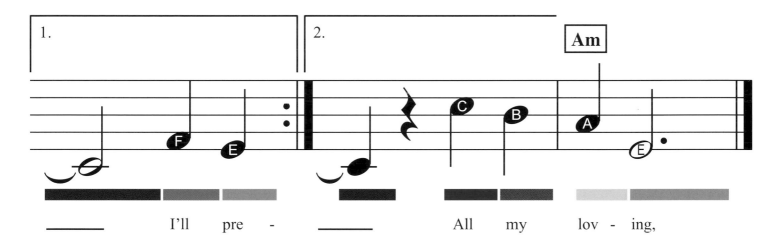

ABC

Words and Music by ALPHONSO MIZELL,
FREDERICK PERREN, DEKE RICHARDS
and BERRY GORDY

Registration 9
Rhythm: Rock or 8-Beat

THE BALLAD OF DAVY CROCKETT
from Walt Disney's DAVY CROCKETT

Words by TOM BLACKBURN
Music by GEORGE BRUNS

Registration 2
Rhythm: Fox Trot or Swing

ALL MY LOVING

Words and Music by JOHN LENNON
and PAUL McCARTNEY

Registration 9
Rhythm: Rock

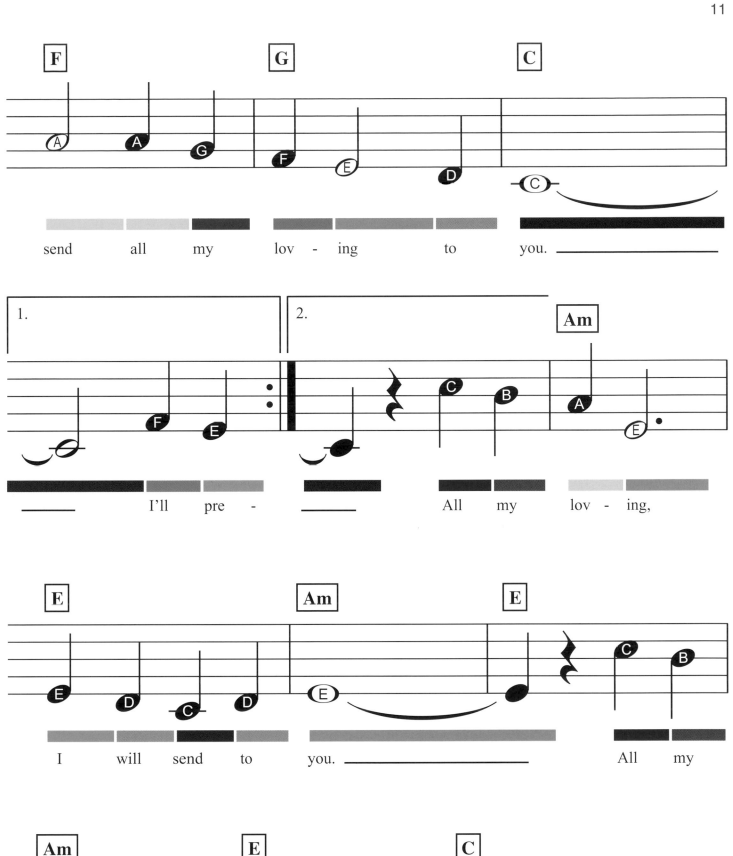

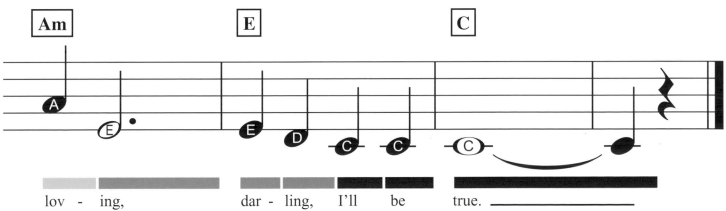

THE BARE NECESSITIES
from Walt Disney's THE JUNGLE BOOK

Words and Music by
TERRY GILKYSON

Registration 4
Rhythm: Fox Trot or Swing

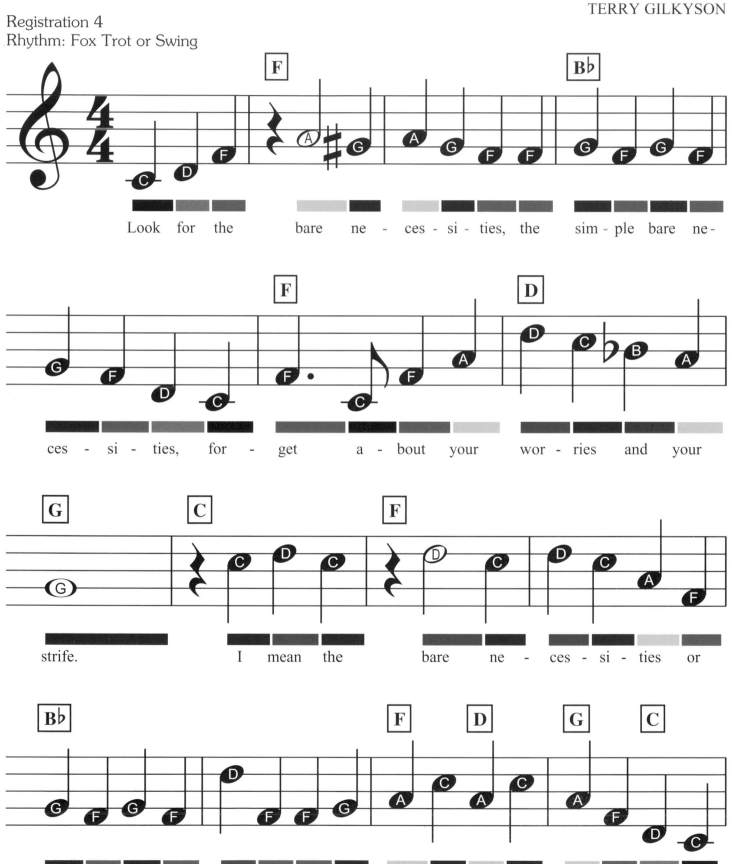

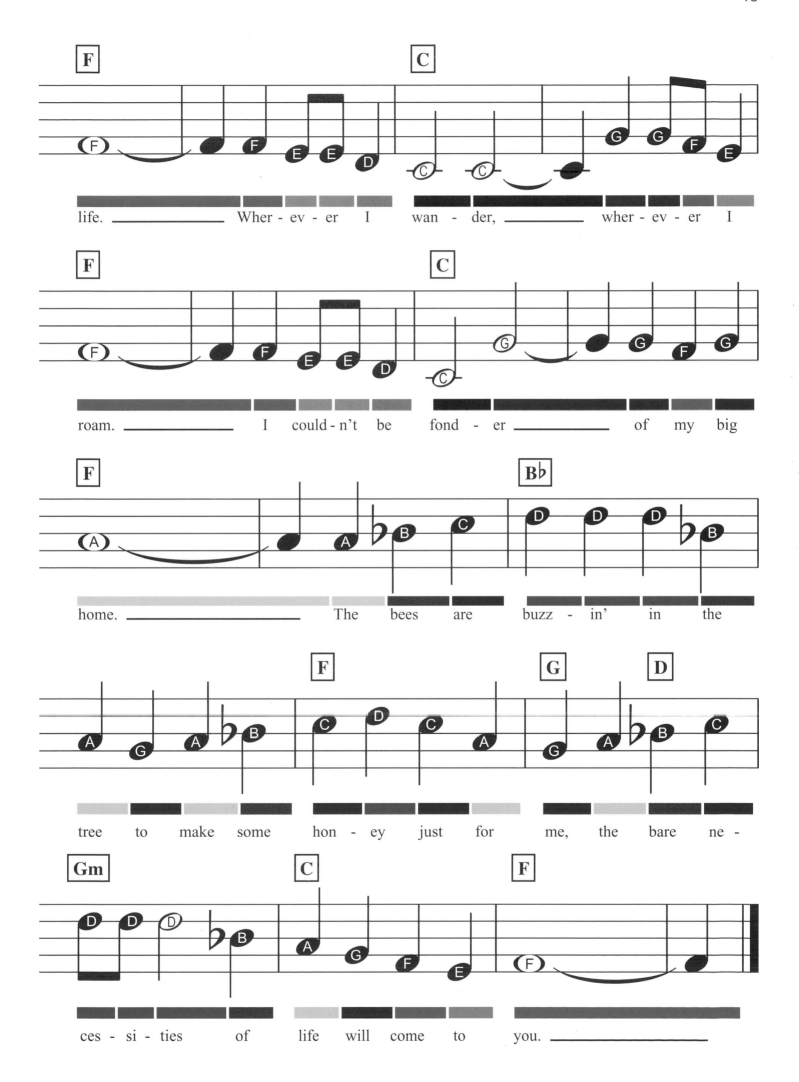

Musical Words

There are many words that use just the seven letters of the musical alphabet. You might say they are "musical words." Here are some of them. Fill in the blanks below each note to make a musical word. In case you get stuck, there's a clue below each word.

After you've filled in the blanks, play each word to hear how it sounds musically. Also, try putting different words together to form complete "musical sentences."

3 Letter Words

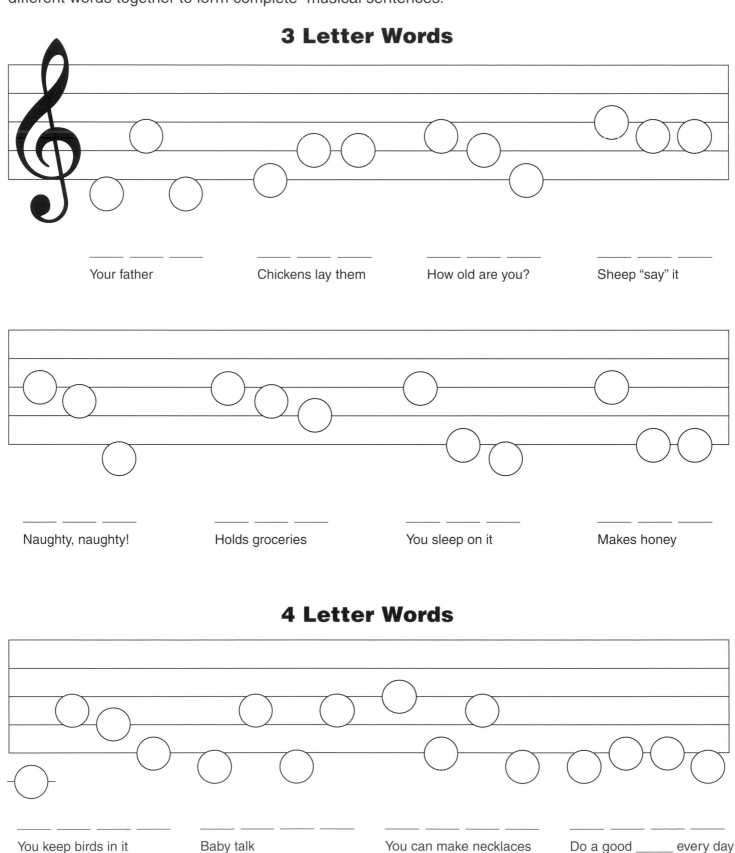

___ ___ ___   ___ ___ ___   ___ ___ ___   ___ ___ ___
Your father   Chickens lay them   How old are you?   Sheep "say" it

___ ___ ___   ___ ___ ___   ___ ___ ___   ___ ___ ___
Naughty, naughty!   Holds groceries   You sleep on it   Makes honey

4 Letter Words

___ ___ ___ ___   ___ ___ ___ ___   ___ ___ ___ ___   ___ ___ ___ ___
You keep birds in it   Baby talk   You can make necklaces   Do a good ____ every day
                                                from them

This page is a little tricky. Now, try the following section without the hints to help you. Fill in the letter to create a word – check your answers on page 88.

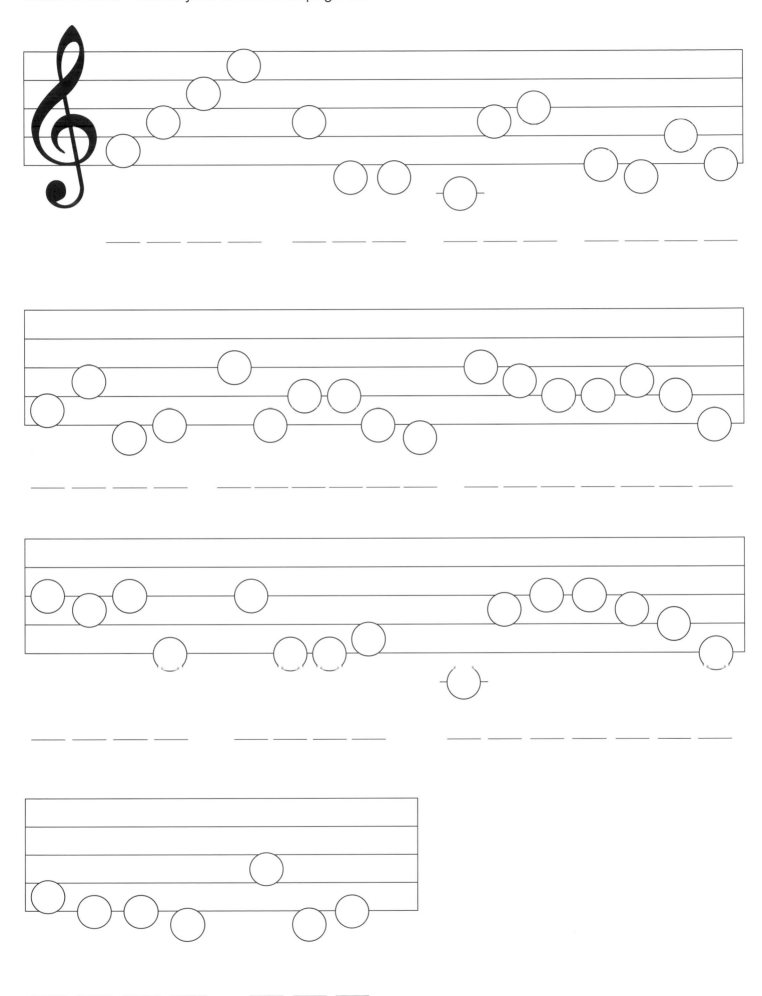

BROWN EYED GIRL

Words and Music by
VAN MORRISON

Registration 1
Rhythm: 8-Beat or Rock

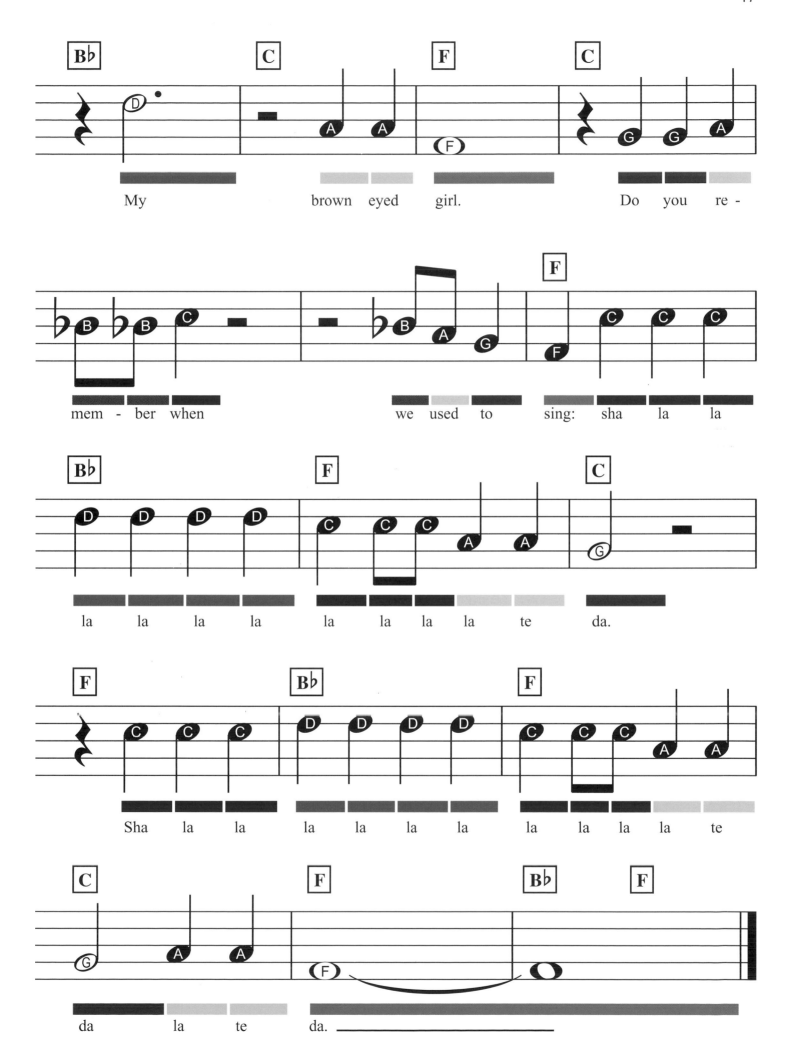

CANDLE ON THE WATER
from Walt Disney's PETE'S DRAGON

Words and Music by AL KASHA
and JOEL HIRSCHHORN

Registration 1
Rhythm: Fox Trot or Ballad

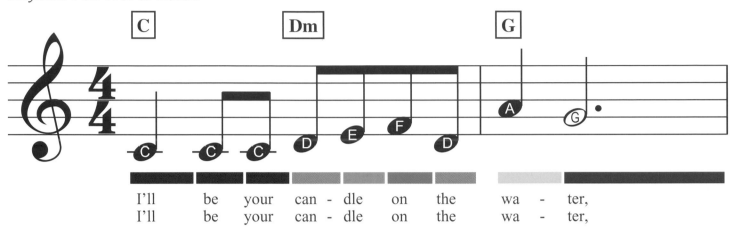

I'll be your can - dle on the wa - ter,
I'll be your can - dle on the wa - ter,

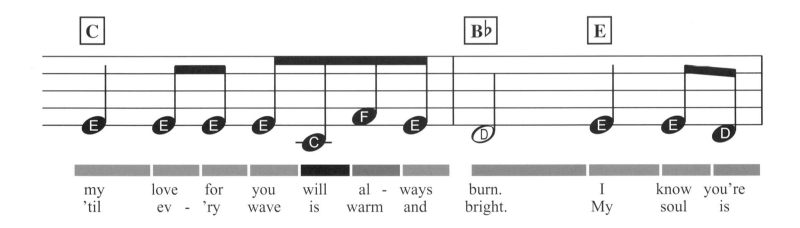

my love for you will al - ways burn. I know you're
'til ev - 'ry wave is warm and bright. My soul is

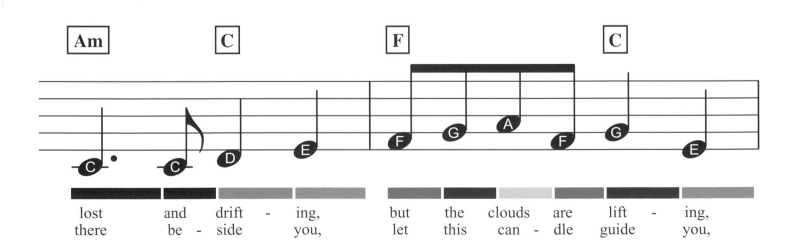

lost and drift - ing, but the clouds are lift - ing,
there be - side you, let this can - dle guide you,

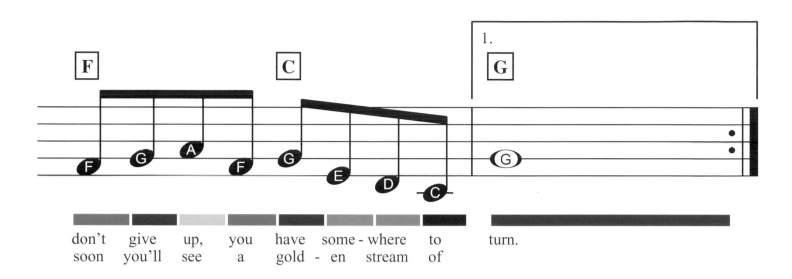

don't give up, you have some - where to turn.
soon you'll see a gold - en stream of

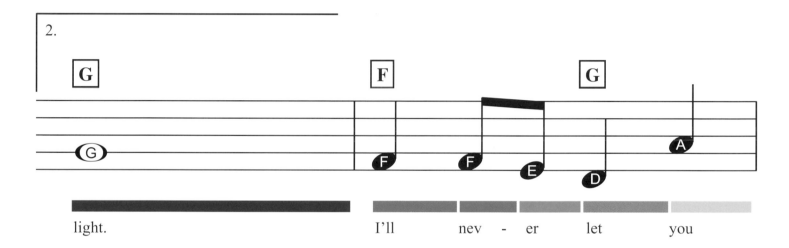

light. I'll nev - er let you

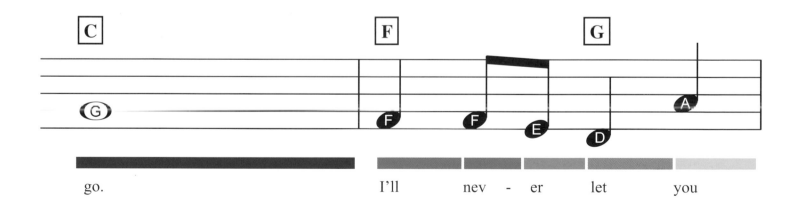

go. I'll nev - er let you

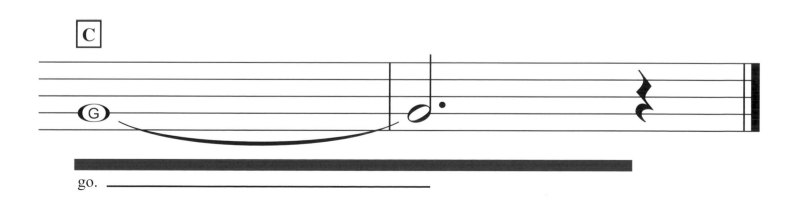

go.

CASPER THE FRIENDLY GHOST
from the Paramount Cartoon

Registration 1
Rhythm: Polka, Rock or March

Words by MACK DAVID
Music by JERRY LIVINGSTON

21

COUNT YOUR BLESSINGS
INSTEAD OF SHEEP
from the Motion Picture Irving Berlin's WHITE CHRISTMAS

Words and Music by
IRVING BERLIN

Registration 4
Rhythm: Swing

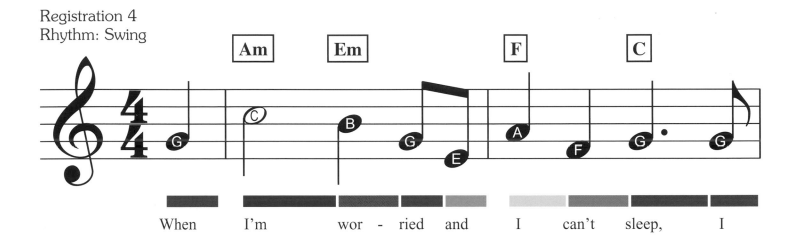

When I'm wor - ried and I can't sleep, I

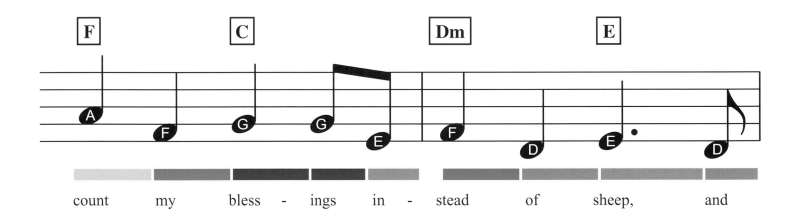

count my bless - ings in - stead of sheep, and

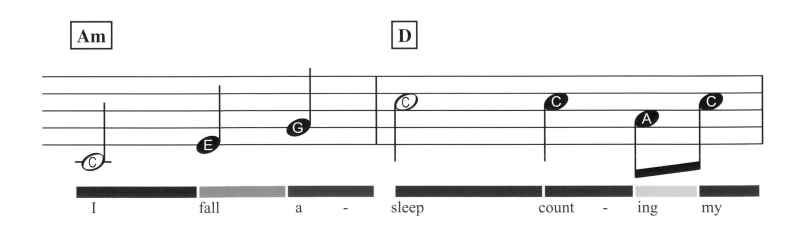

I fall a - sleep count - ing my

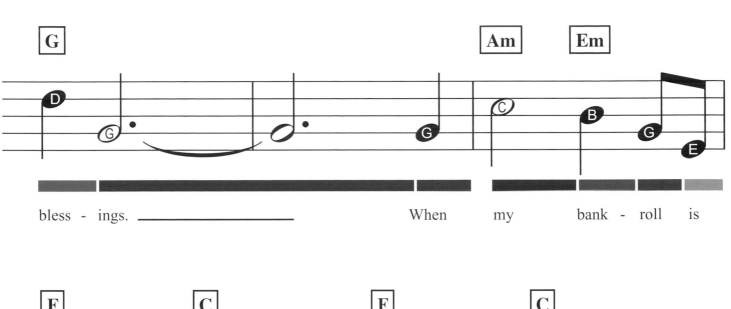

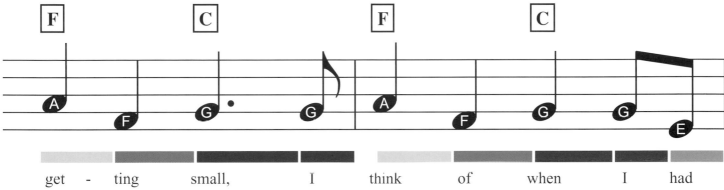

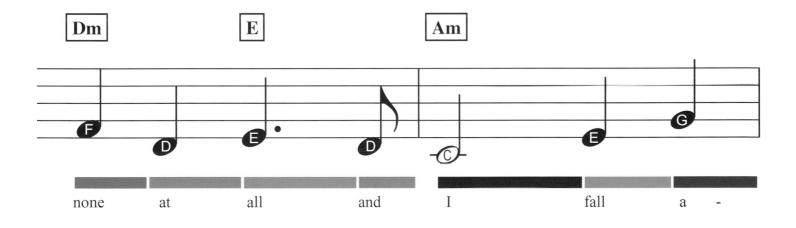

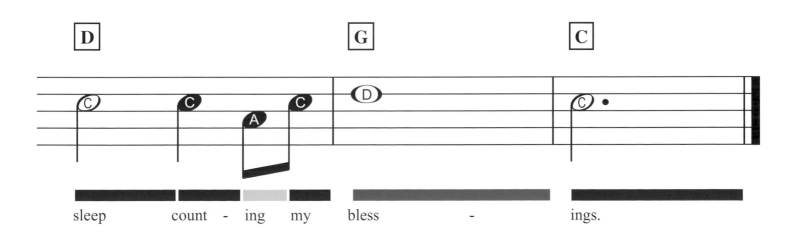

Crossword Fun

ACROSS

2. The bottom number of a time signature tells you what kind of note is one _____ long.

4. A _____ note lasts two beats.

6. You can divide a whole note into smaller pieces, just like a pepperoni _____.

7. A treble _____ appears at the beginning of a song.

9. Music _____ are written on the lines and spaces of the staff.

13. A whole note lasts _____ beats.

14. Black notes are short. White notes are _____.

15. The letter names of the spaces on the treble staff, from bottom to top, spell this word.

16. A _____ is the space between two bar lines.

18. The top number of a time signature tells you how many _____ are in a measure.

DOWN

1. Notes that are too high or too low to fit on the staff are written using ledger _____.

2. A double _____ tells you where the song ends.

3. In ¾ time there are _____ beats in every measure.

5. The letters in the music alphabet are: _____.

8. The _____ half note lasts for three beats.

10. White notes are long. Black notes are _____.

11. In ¼ time the _____ note is one beat long.

12. Notes are written on the _____, which has five lines.

17. There are _____ letters in the music alphabet.

Answers on p. 88

DON'T BE CRUEL
(To a Heart That's True)

Words and Music by OTIS BLACKWELL
and ELVIS PRESLEY

Registration 4
Rhythm: Rock

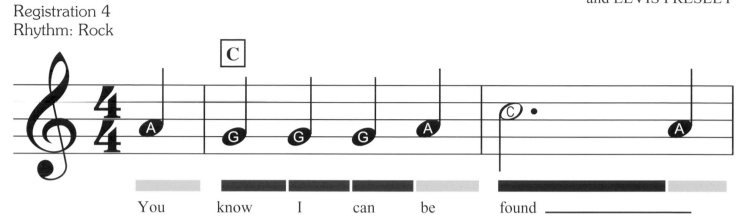

You know I can be found ____

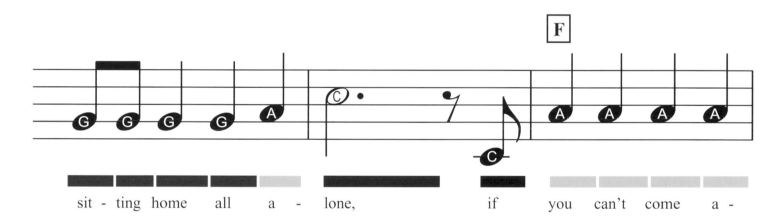

sit - ting home all a - lone, if you can't come a -

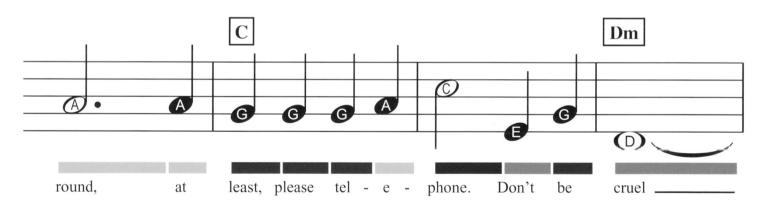

round, at least, please tel - e - phone. Don't be cruel ____

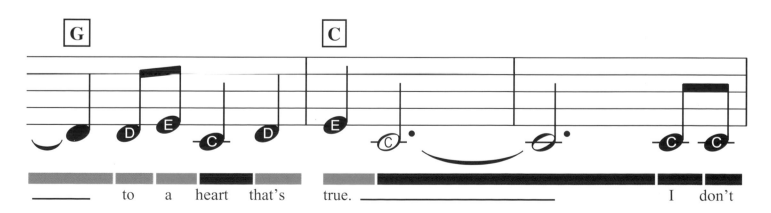

____ to a heart that's true. ____ I don't

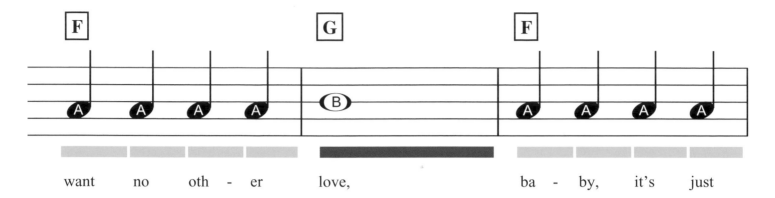

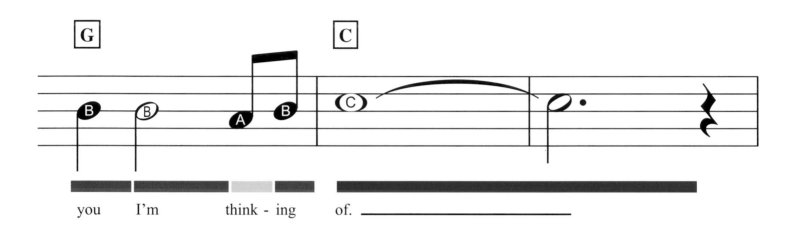

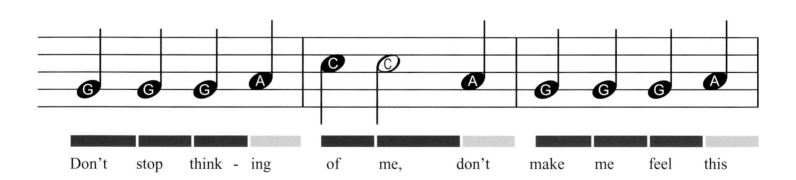

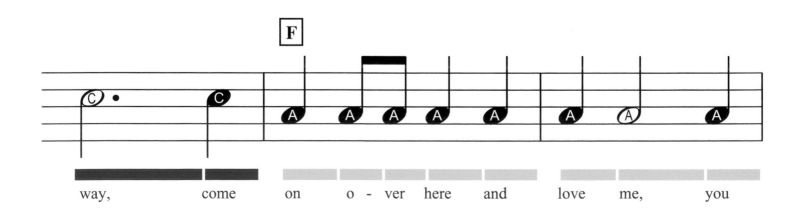

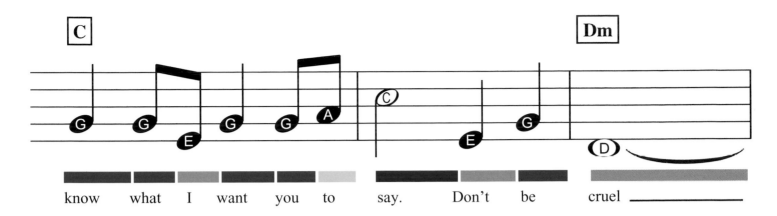

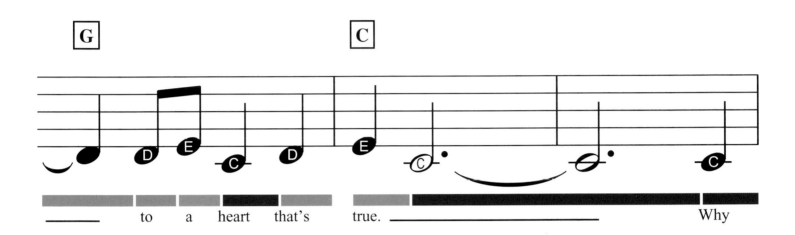

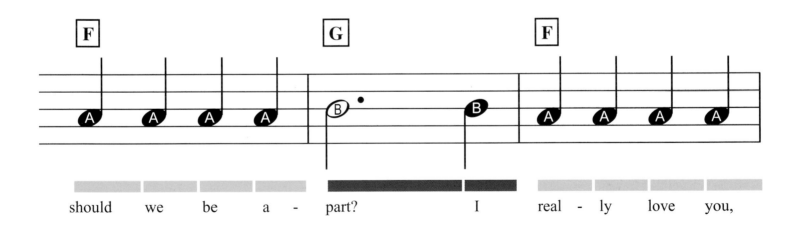

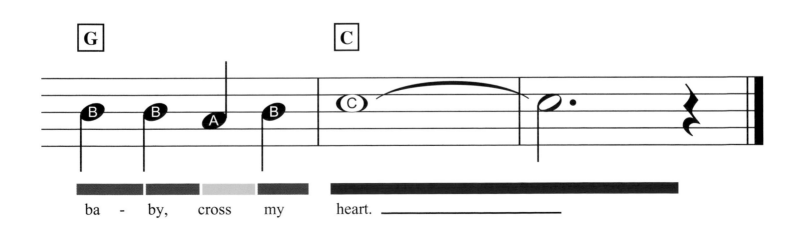

DO-RE-MI
from THE SOUND OF MUSIC

Lyrics by OSCAR HAMMERSTEIN II
Music by RICHARD RODGERS

Registration 4
Rhythm: March

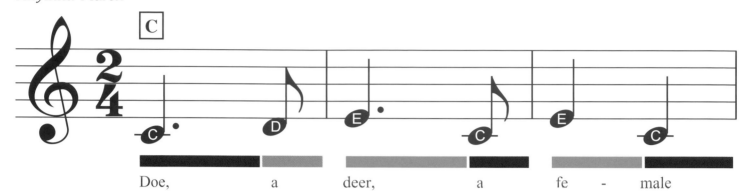

Doe, a deer, a fe - male

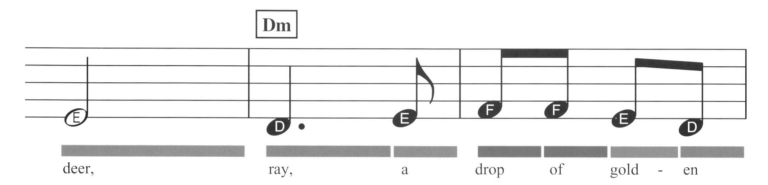

deer, ray, a drop of gold - en

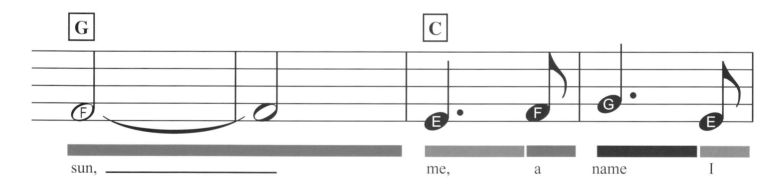

sun, me, a name I

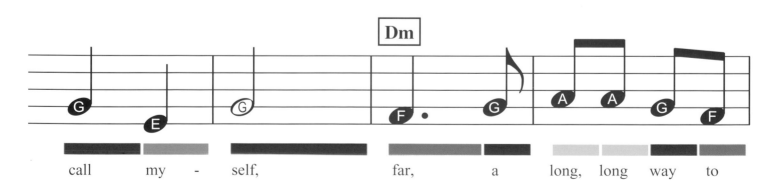

call my - self, far, a long, long way to

EVERYTHING IS BEAUTIFUL

Words and Music by
RAY STEVENS

Registration 8
Rhythm: Rock or Jazz Rock

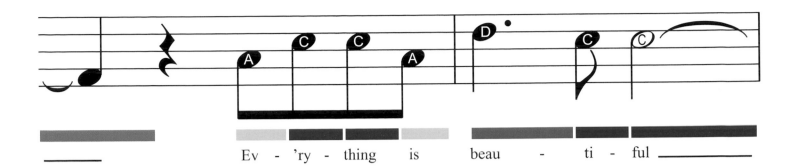

Ev - 'ry - thing is beau - ti - ful

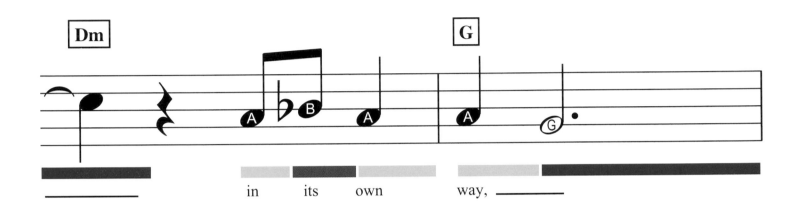

Dm   **G**

in its own way,

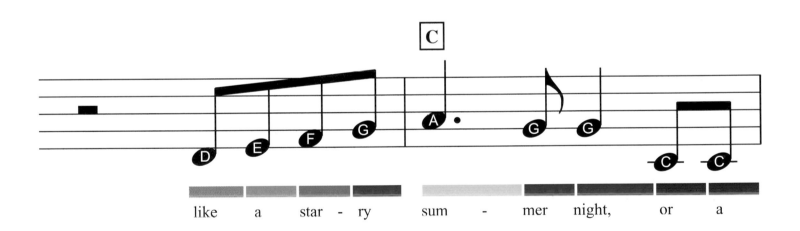

C

like a star - ry sum - mer night, or a

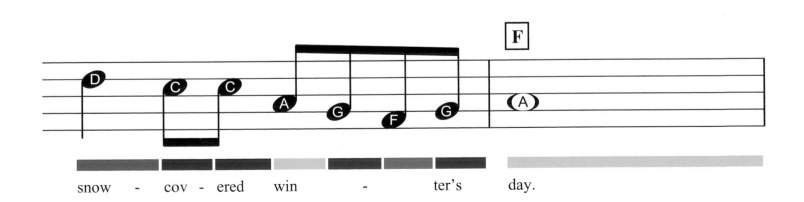

F

snow - cov - ered win - ter's day.

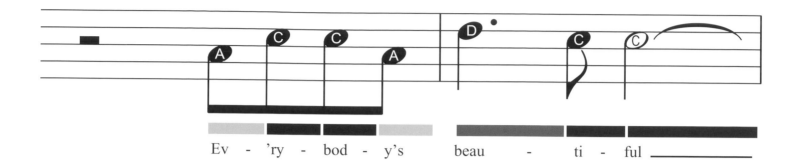

Ev - 'ry - bod - y's beau - ti - ful _____

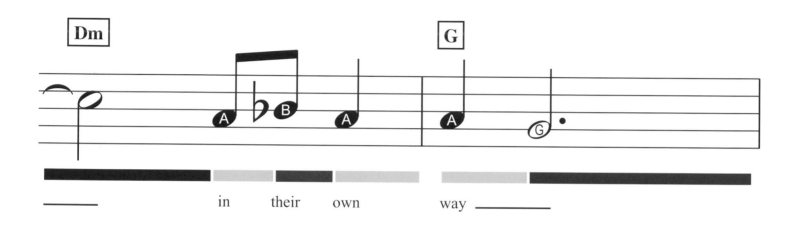

_____ in their own way _____

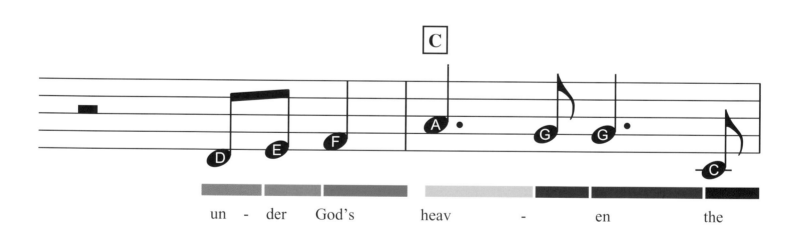

un - der God's heav - en the

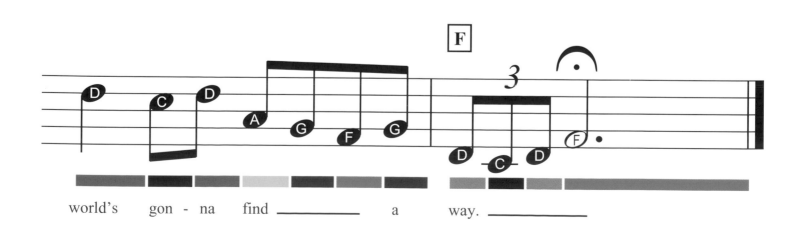

world's gon - na find _____ a way. _____

Connect the Dots

Can you name this symbol?

● 11

● 10   ● 12

● 9
          ● 13

● 8
          ● 14

● 15   ●7

● 16   ● 22
     ● 23

          ● 6   ● 21

●17   ● 24

          ● 25   ● 20
● 18
          ●19

● 1

          ● 5

● 2
          ● 4
● 3

GONNA BUILD A MOUNTAIN
from the Musical Production STOP THE WORLD - I WANT TO GET OFF

Words and Music by LESLIE BRICUSSE
and ANTHONY NEWLEY

Registration 4
Rhythm: Fox Trot

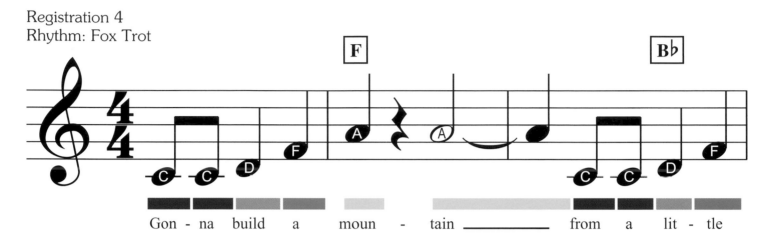

Gon - na build a moun - tain _____ from a lit - tle

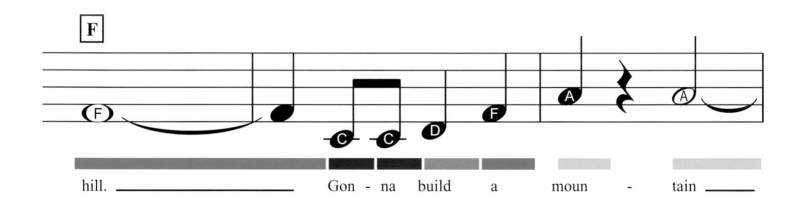

hill. _____ Gon - na build a moun - tain _____

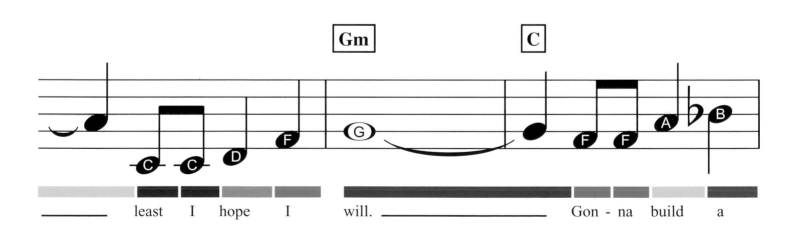

_____ least I hope I will. _____ Gon - na build a

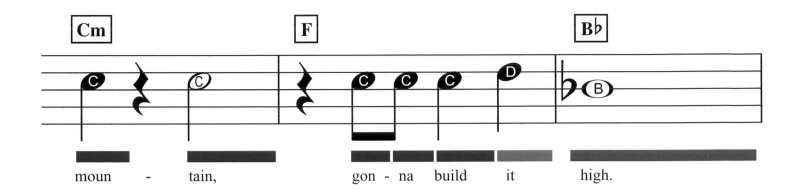

moun - tain,   gon - na   build   it   high.

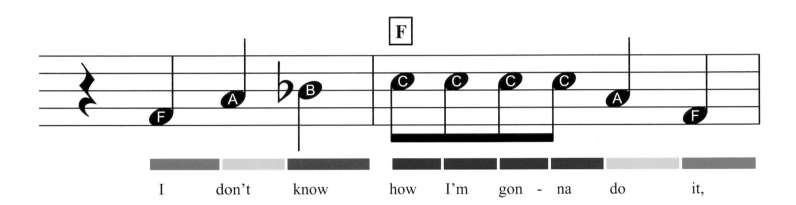

I   don't   know   how   I'm   gon - na   do   it,

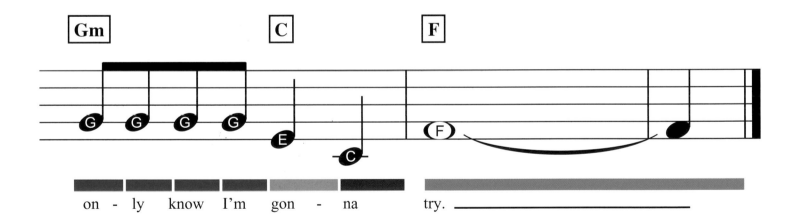

on - ly   know   I'm   gon - na   try. _____

HAPPY BIRTHDAY TO YOU

Words and Music by MILDRED J. HILL
and PATTY S. HILL

Registration 8
Rhythm: Waltz

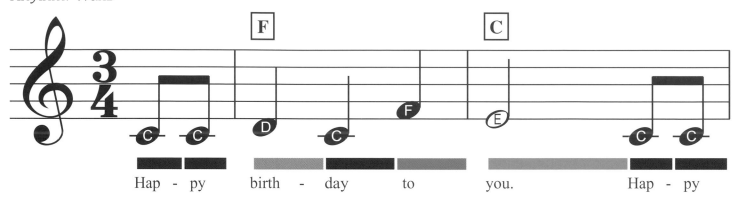

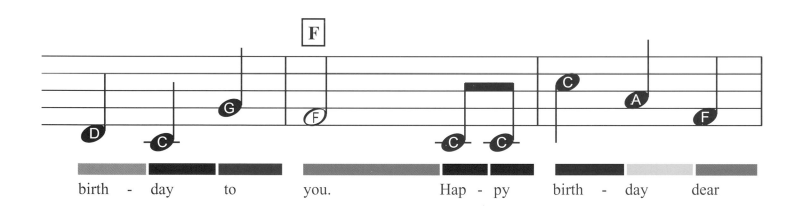

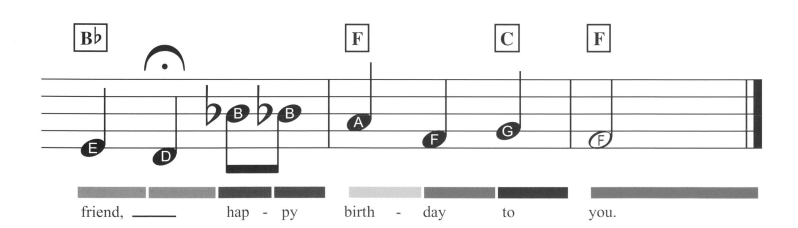

THE HOKEY POKEY

Words and Music by CHARLES P. MACAK,
TAFFT BAKER and LARRY LaPRISE

Registration 5
Rhythm: Fox Trot or Swing

*continue with left hand, right, left shoulder, hip, leg, foot, whole self.

HAPPY TRAILS
from the Television Series THE ROY ROGERS SHOW

Words and Music by
DALE EVANS

Registration 5
Rhythm: Swing or Pops

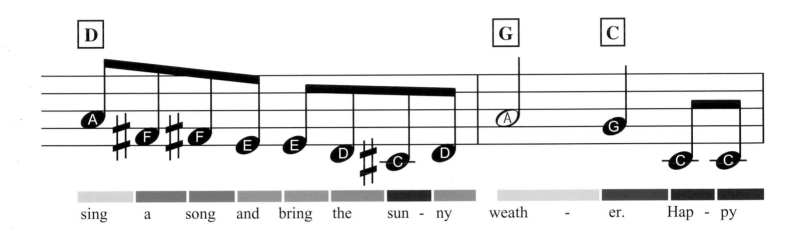

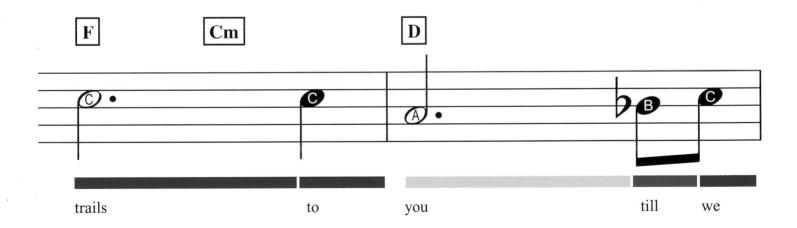

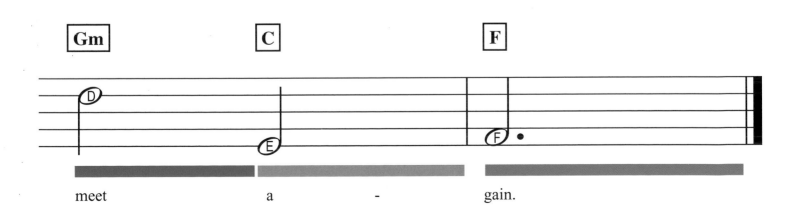

I'M A BELIEVER

Words and Music by
NEIL DIAMOND

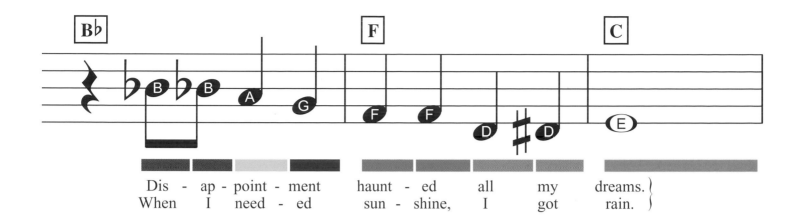

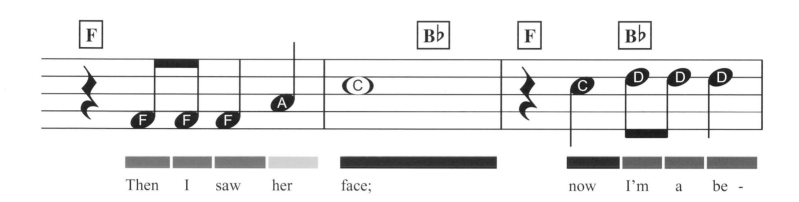

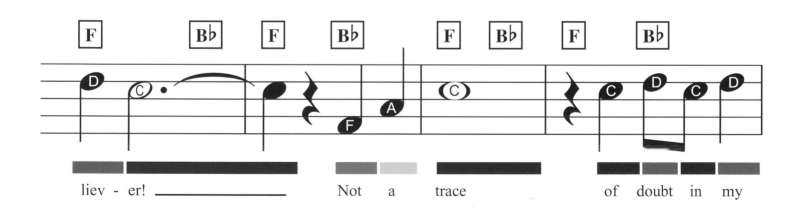

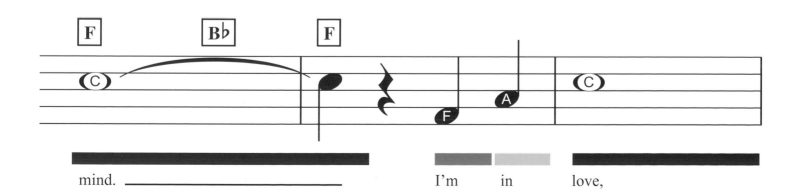

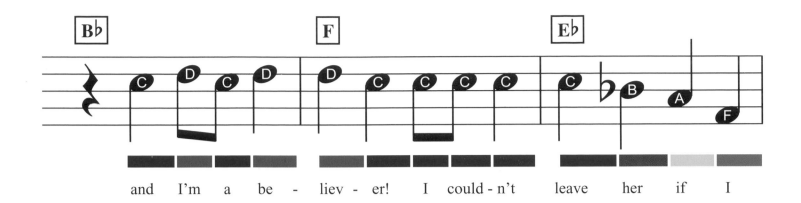

and I'm a be - liev - er! I could - n't leave her if I

tried. _____

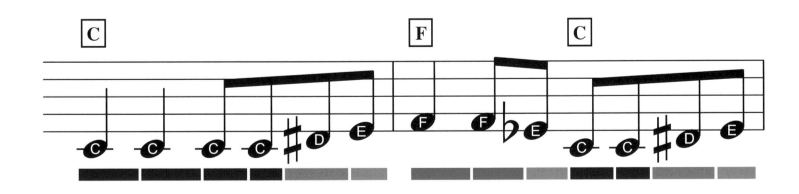

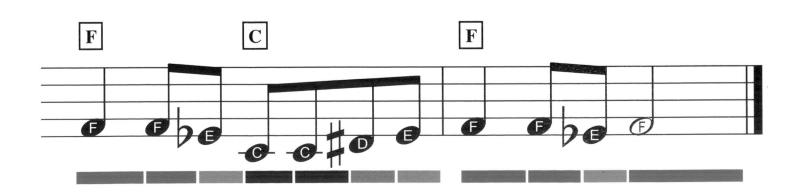

Word Search

Can you find all the music words on the list?
Circle the words you find and then cross them off the list as you work.

```
K Q H D A C A P O Y Q D A S B T I W L V K Q H
E K V O O Z S T G B X C M W O X R G E P X X Z
Y E V P R M W P L H A H C H Q J Z I I E X W O
B L J T E M P O A Z R O Y O M J B T T B B Q I
O U B B B W S I Y C P R V L G G O H A F C X
A D T S N U Q T D N E D X E K V N I Q R R R Y
R Y E U K U B C X O G S T N R D F Z O L E M L
D N B I Z I F O C T G Y Q O E K B S O I S F M
C A O R G W P S K E I M H T X C A P S N T M M
B M T A F H L I T S O B T E E C H K B E T U S
D I Y R O B T U H U O P X O L L Q U S H S O
I C L A E E H H S T D L X T I P T I C A H I W
Q S O R B B S U N H L E D G E R L I N E A C S
U F B S G S L M L O A B G M D K V G K E L A T
A H P A C T B E F T T R I E D G O M K F F L A
R O L L O E E X C P C E P A O F I Y V T N P F
T F M R D P A P C L E K F S U V D M U P O H F
E B B P A G M K S Q E L I U B U Q G T W T A Z
R E P E A T S I G N Z F N R L H Z A N Z E B S
N O S D A P A L H P V N E E E A L W M F H E C
O U V H X T Y F S C A L E J B F Z T Q X S T V
T H T I E K L O L U G J R M A A S B V R T E U
E T I M E S I G N A T U R E R C Y J R T L I Q
```

Arpeggio, Bar lines, Beam, Beat, Chord symbol, Coda, Da capo, Dotted note, Double bar, Dynamics, Eighth note, Fine, Flag, Flat, Half note, Keyboard, Ledger line, Line, Measure, Music alphabet, Notes, Quarter note, Repeat sign, Rest, Rit, Scale, Sharp, Skip, Space, Staff, Step, Tempo, Tie, Time signature, Treble clef, Whole note

I'D LIKE TO TEACH THE WORLD TO SING

Words and Music by BILL BACKER,
ROQUEL DAVIS, ROGER COOK
and ROGER GREENAWAY

Registration 8
Rhythm: Swing

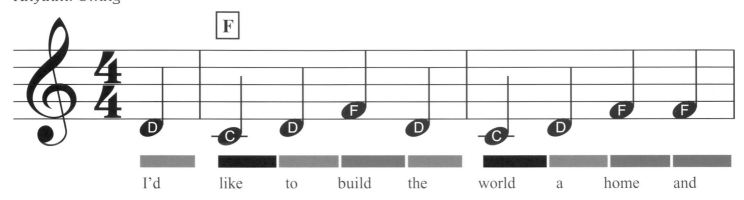

I'd like to build the world a home and

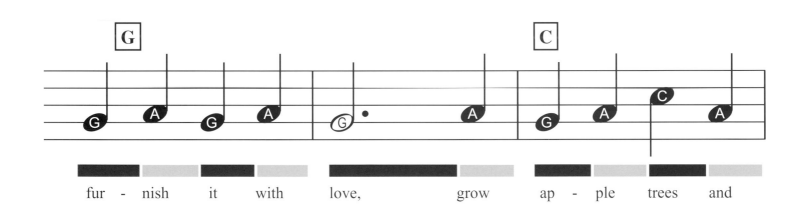

fur - nish it with love, grow ap - ple trees and

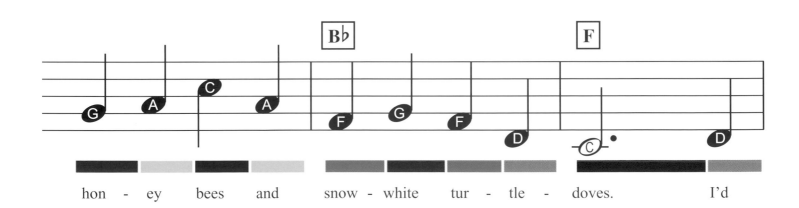

hon - ey bees and snow - white tur - tle - doves. I'd

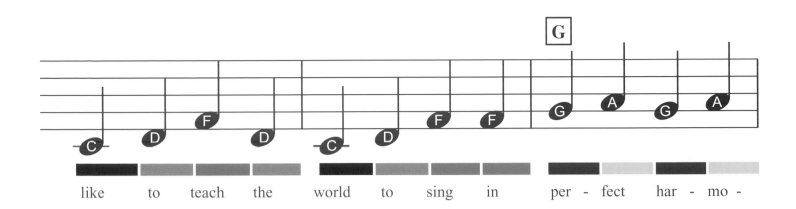

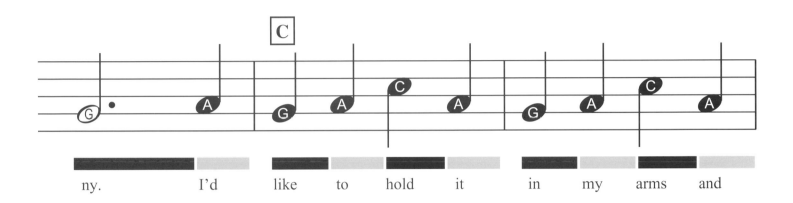

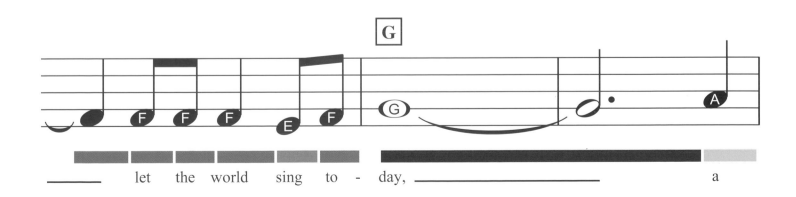

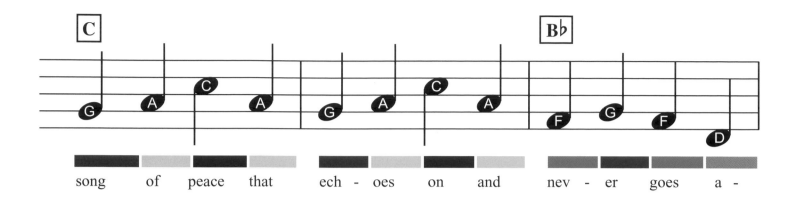

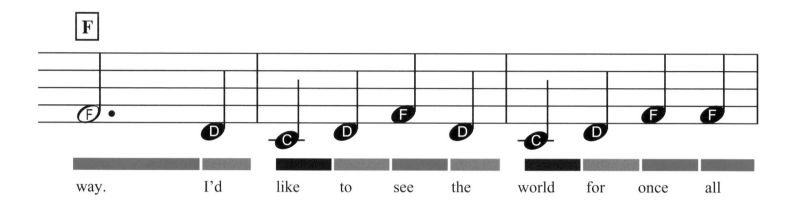

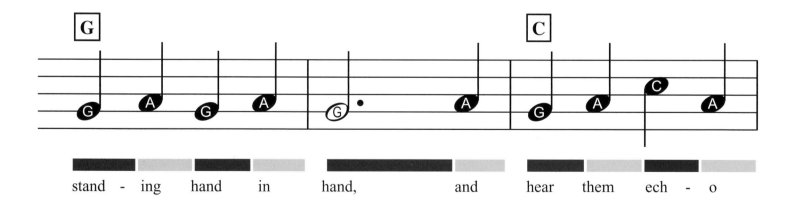

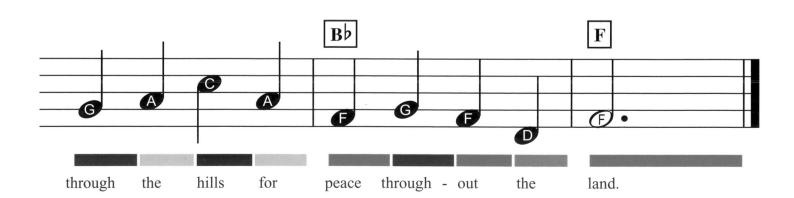

LET THE SUNSHINE IN
from the Broadway Musical Production HAIR

Words by JAMES RADO and GEROME RAGNI
Music by GALT MacDERMOT

Registration 4
Rhythm: Rock or 8 Beat

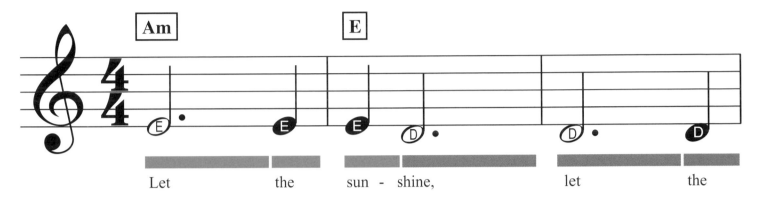

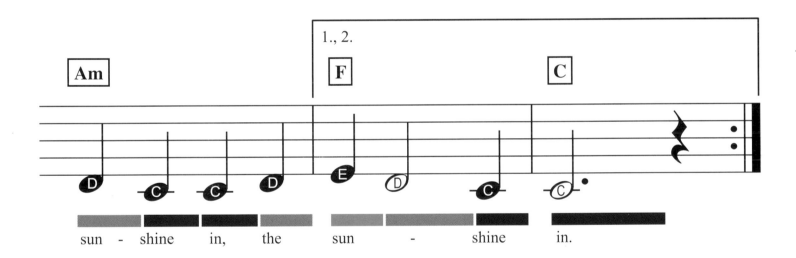

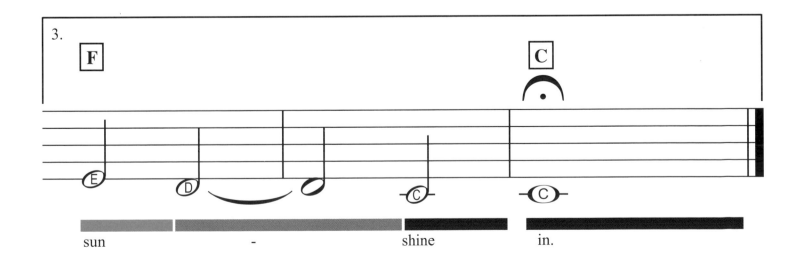

IF I HAD A HAMMER
(The Hammer Song)

Words and Music by LEE HAYS
and PETE SEEGER

Registration 5
Rhythm: Rock or Fox Trot

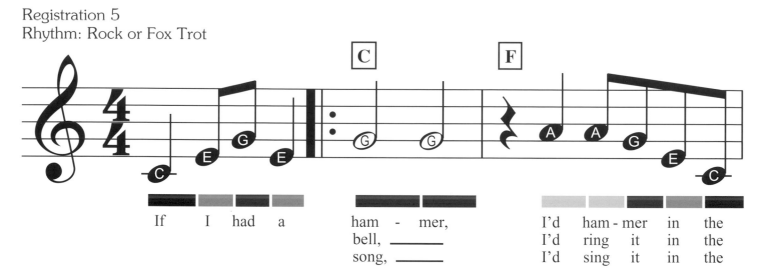

If I had a hammer,   I'd ham-mer in the
bell, _____   I'd ring it in the
song, _____   I'd sing it in the

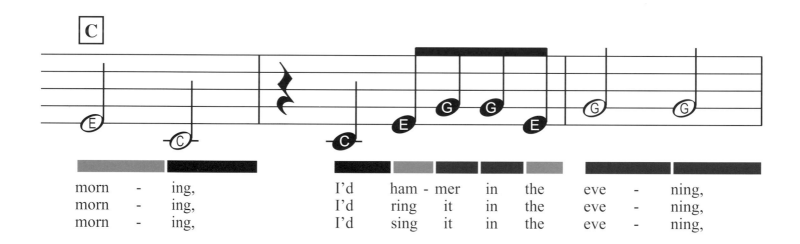

morn - ing,   I'd ham-mer in the eve - ning,
morn - ing,   I'd ring it in the eve - ning,
morn - ing,   I'd sing it in the eve - ning,

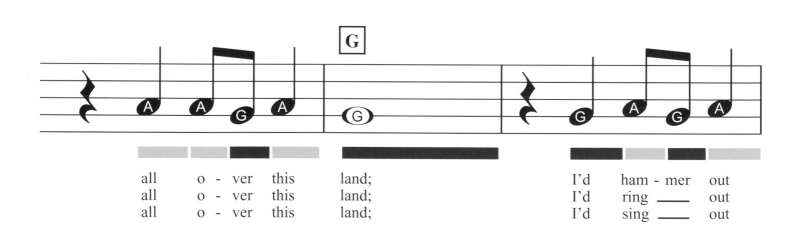

all   o - ver this   land;   I'd ham-mer out
all   o - ver this   land;   I'd ring ____ out
all   o - ver this   land;   I'd sing ____ out

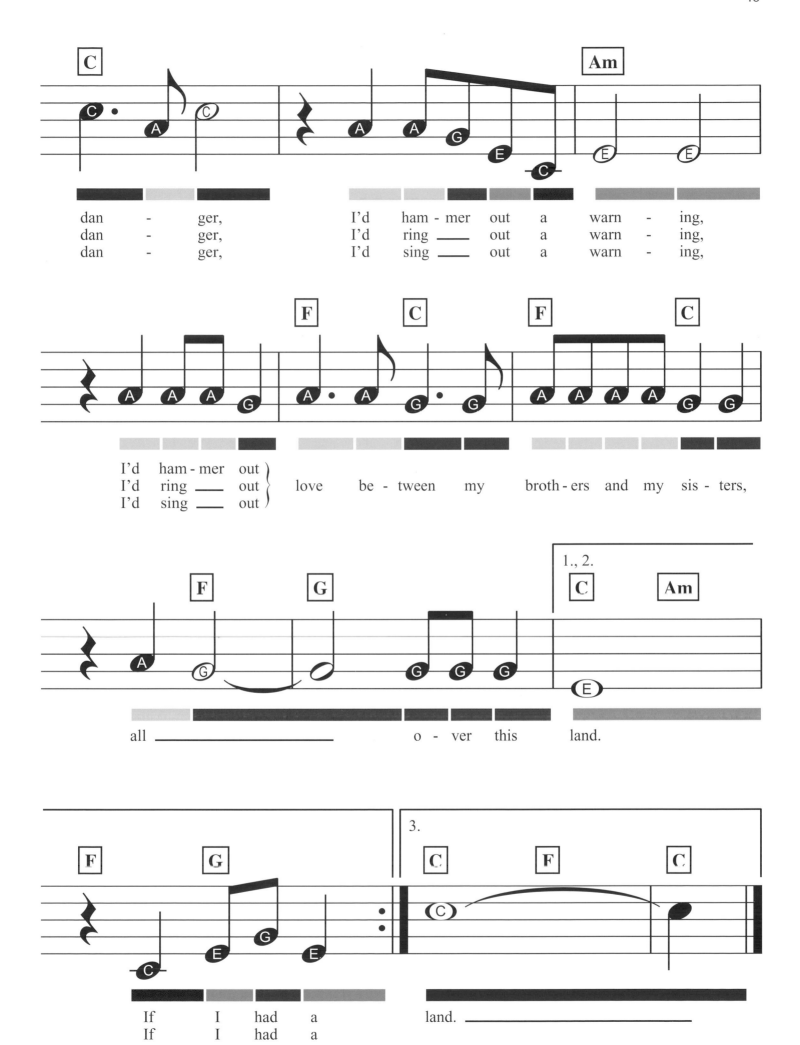

LEAN ON ME

Words and Music by
BILL WITHERS

Registration 8
Rhythm: Rock or 8-Beat

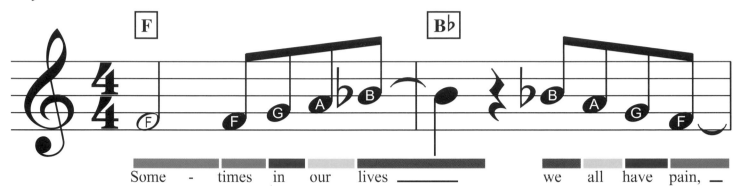

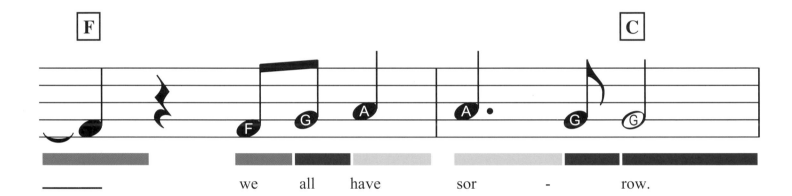

Some - times in our lives _____ we all have pain, ___

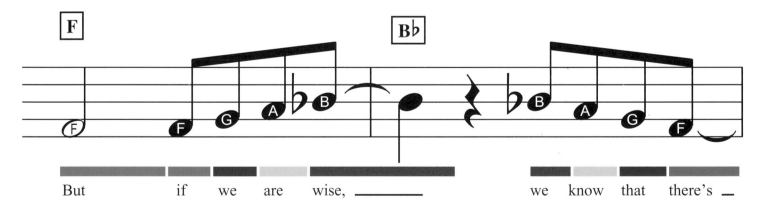

_____ we all have sor - row.

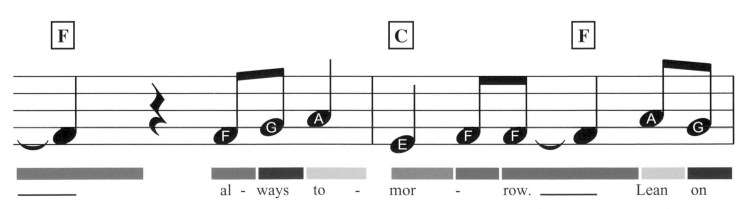

But if we are wise, _____ we know that there's ___

_____ al - ways to - mor - row. _____ Lean on

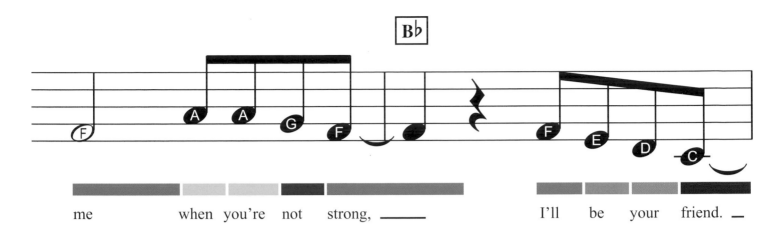

me   when you're not strong, _____   I'll   be   your   friend. __

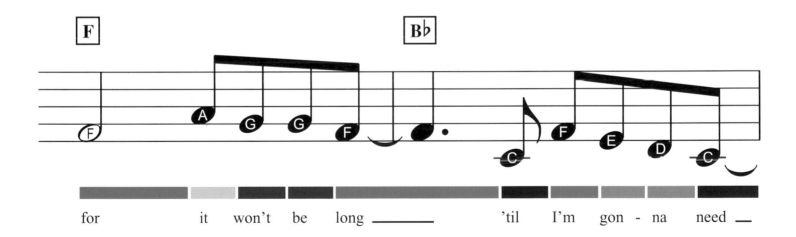

_____   I'll   help   you   car - ry   on, _____

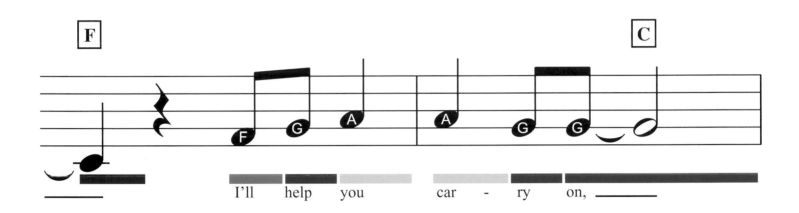

for   it   won't   be   long _____   'til   I'm   gon - na   need __

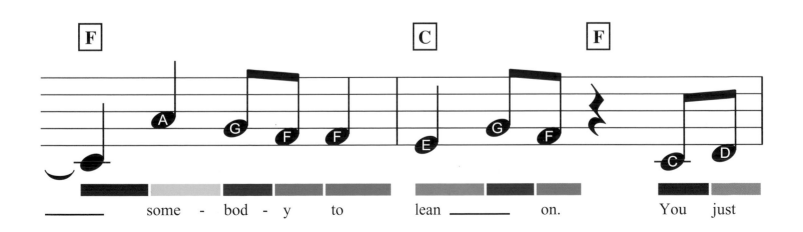

_____   some - bod - y   to   lean _____   on.   You   just

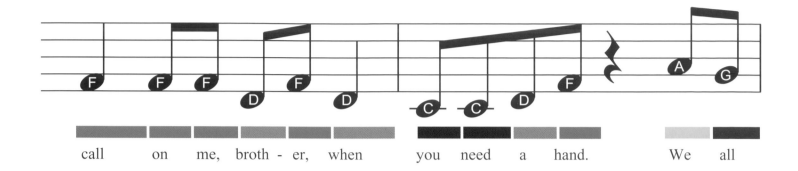

call on me, broth - er, when you need a hand. We all

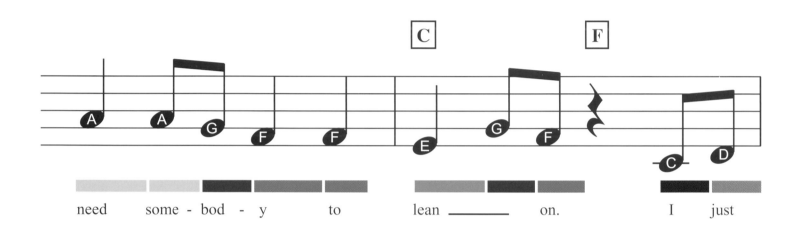

need some - bod - y to lean _____ on. I just

C   F

might have a prob - lem that you'll un - der - stand. We all

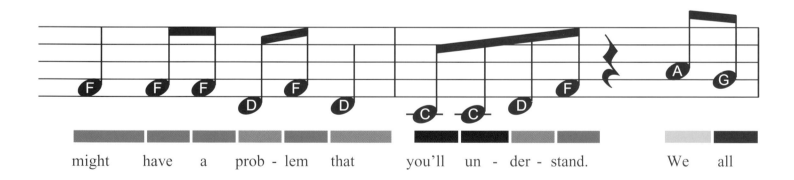

need some - bod - y to lean _____ on.

C   F

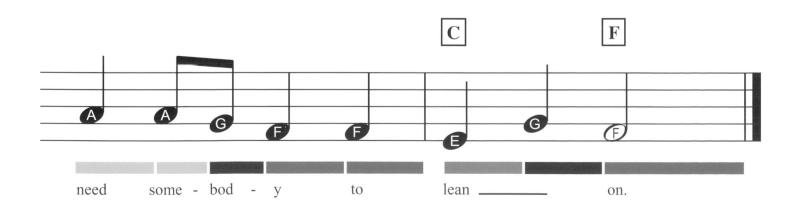

Note Reading Review

Name the notes and color the fish with crayons, pencils or markers
using the note and color key at the bottom of the page.

light blue   yellow   orange   dark blue   green   red   pink

LINUS AND LUCY

By VINCE GUARALDI

Registration 8
Rhythm: Fox Trot or Swing

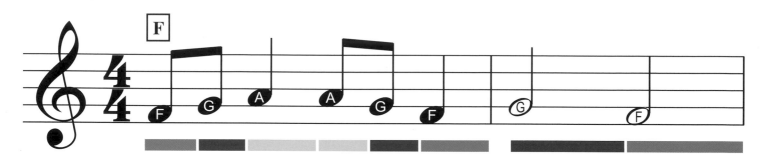

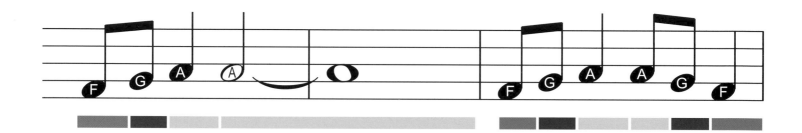

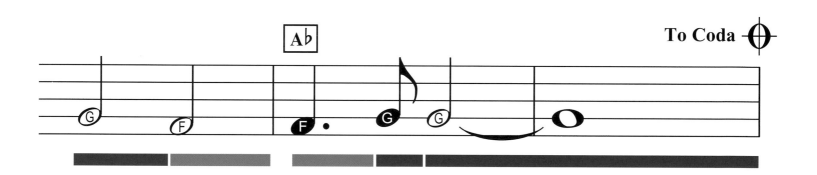

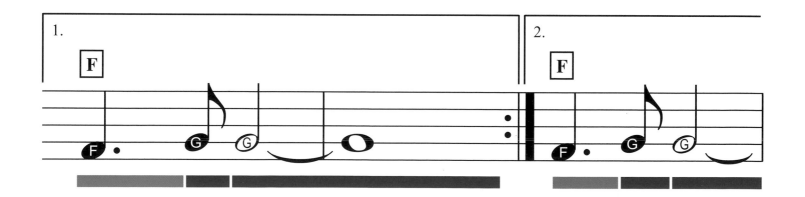

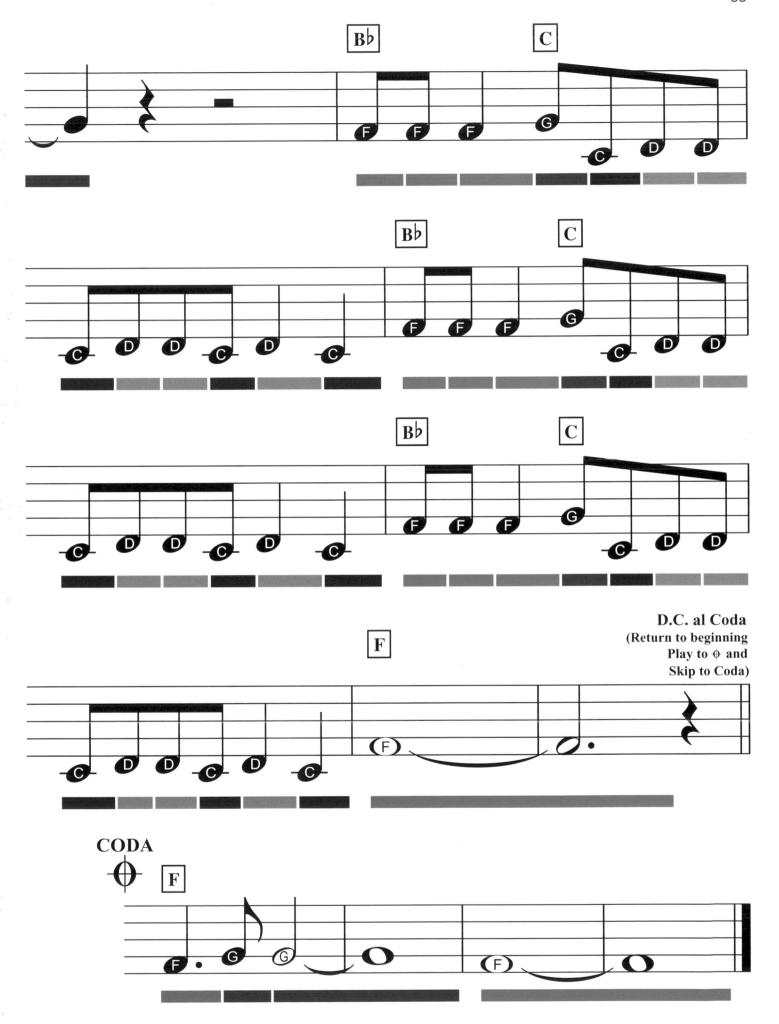

THE MARVELOUS TOY

Words and Music by
TOM PAXTON

Registration 5
Rhythm: Pops, Fox Trot or March

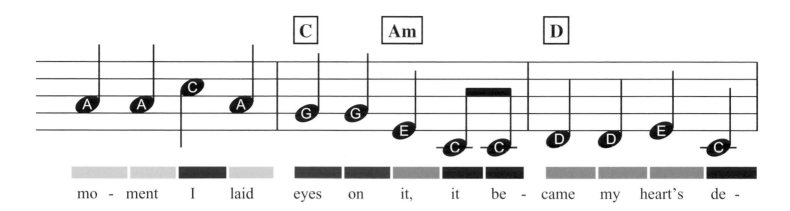

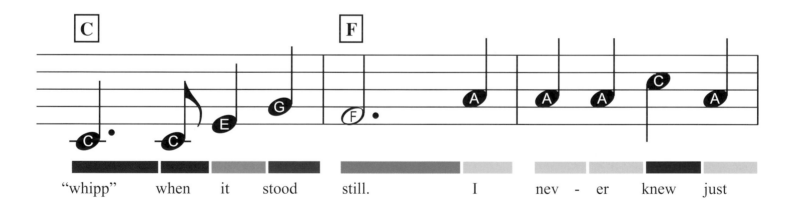

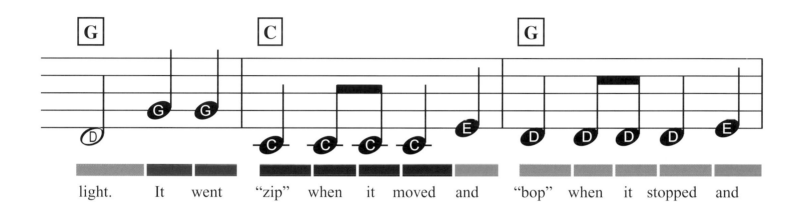

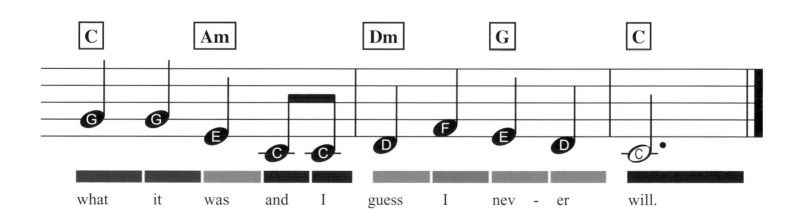

ME AND YOU AND A DOG NAMED BOO

Words and Music by
LOBO

Registration 1
Rhythm: Rock, March or Polka

I re - mem - ber to this day the bright red Geor - gia clay, how it stuck to the tires af - ter the sum - mer rain. _____ Will - pow - er made that old car go, a wom - an's

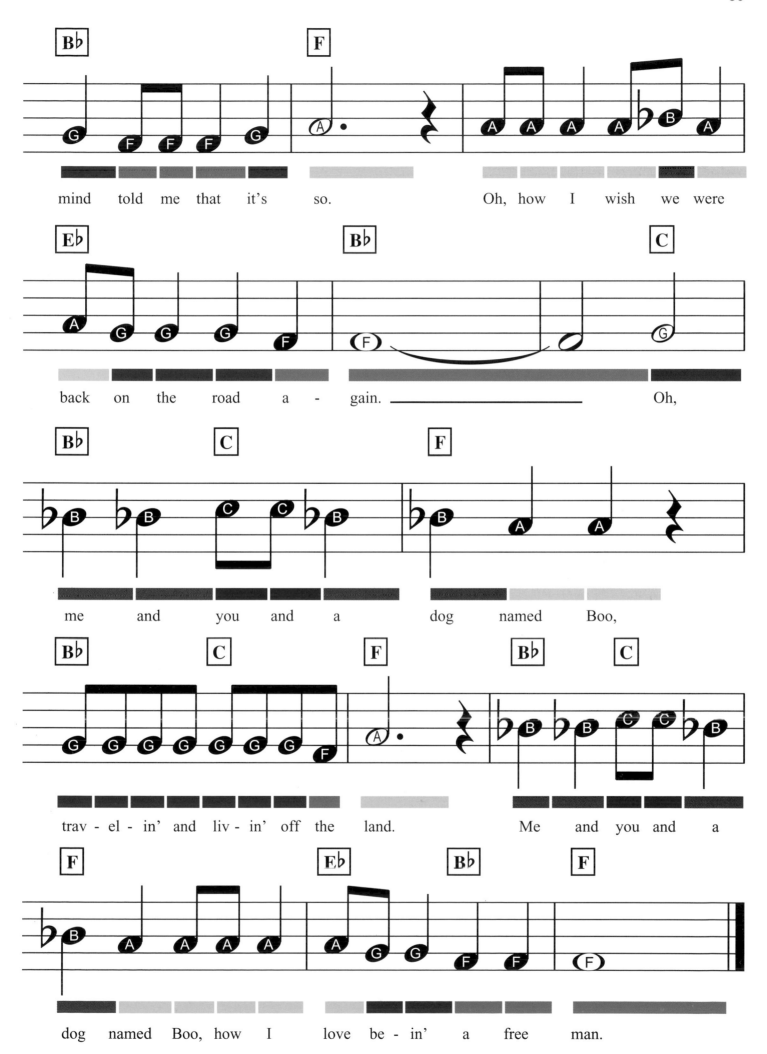

THE MEDALLION CALLS
from Walt Disney Pictures' PIRATES OF THE CARIBBEAN:
THE CURSE OF THE BLACK PEARL

Words and Music by
KLAUS BADELT

Registration 2
Rhythm: Waltz

Music Math

Let's do some music math! Add the values of the tied notes to find the
answer to each of these musical equations. The first one is done for you.
Check your answers on page 88.

1.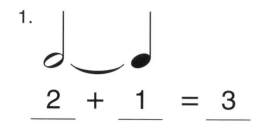

$\underline{\ 2\ } + \underline{\ 1\ } = \underline{\ 3\ }$

2.

$\underline{\quad} + \underline{\quad} + \underline{\quad} = \underline{\quad}$

3.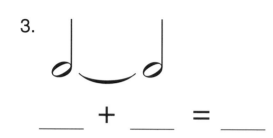

$\underline{\quad} + \underline{\quad} = \underline{\quad}$

4.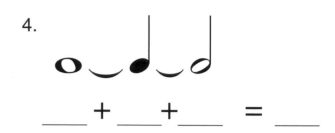

$\underline{\quad} + \underline{\quad} + \underline{\quad} = \underline{\quad}$

5.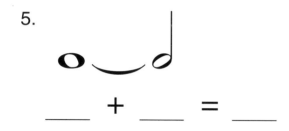

$\underline{\quad} + \underline{\quad} = \underline{\quad}$

6.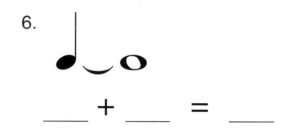

$\underline{\quad} + \underline{\quad} = \underline{\quad}$

7.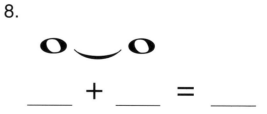

$\underline{\quad} + \underline{\quad} + \underline{\quad} = \underline{\quad}$

8.

$\underline{\quad} + \underline{\quad} = \underline{\quad}$

9.

$\underline{\quad} + \underline{\quad} + \underline{\quad} + \underline{\quad} = \underline{\quad}$

10.

$\underline{\quad} + \underline{\quad} + \underline{\quad} + \underline{\quad} = \underline{\quad}$

Find the Hidden Objects

As you color this picture, find the following musical objects:

half note	keyboard	trumpet	treble clef
quarter note	sharp sign	staff	violin
guitar	flat sign	xylophone	drumsticks
	drum	saxophone	

ON THE GOOD SHIP LOLLIPOP
from BRIGHT EYES

Words and Music by SIDNEY CLARE
and RICHARD A. WHITING

Registration 3
Rhythm: Fox Trot or Swing

PETER COTTONTAIL

Words and Music by STEVE NELSON
and JACK ROLLINS

Registration 1
Rhythm: Fox Trot

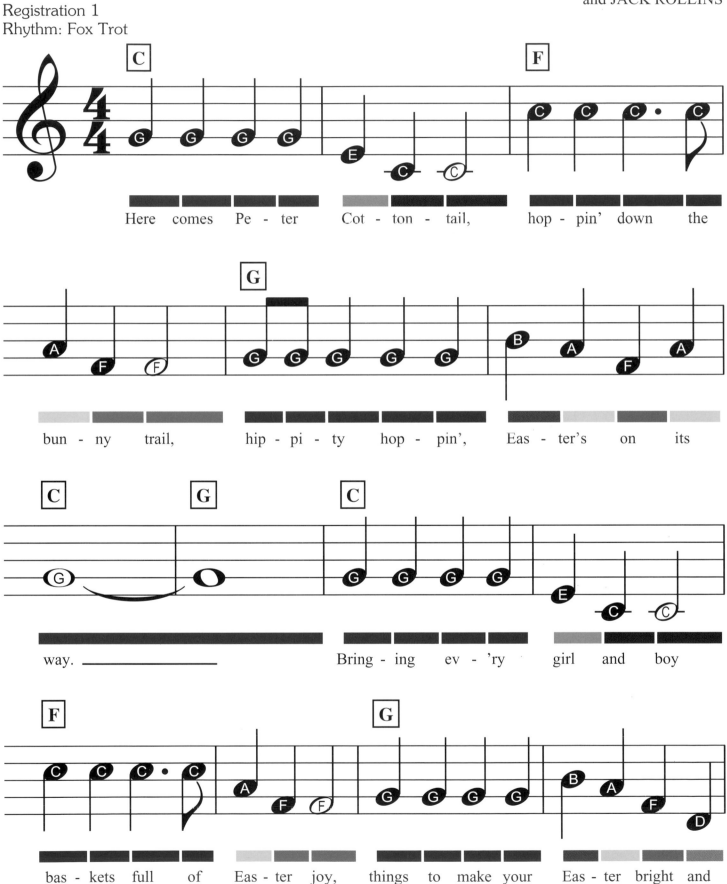

THE RAINBOW CONNECTION
from THE MUPPET MOVIE

Words and Music by PAUL WILLIAMS
and KENNETH L. ASCHER

Registration 4
Rhythm: Waltz

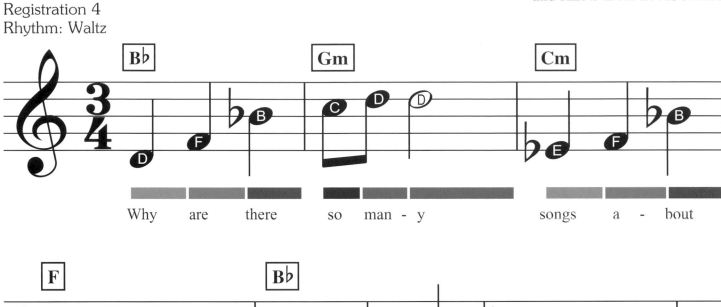

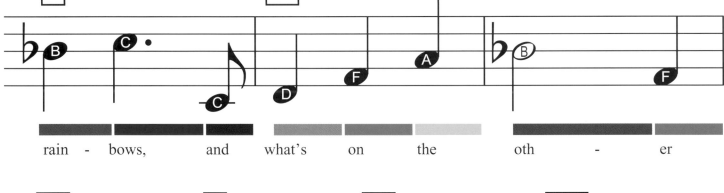

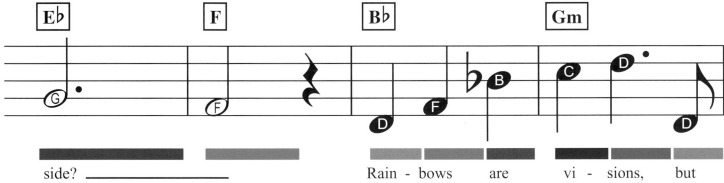

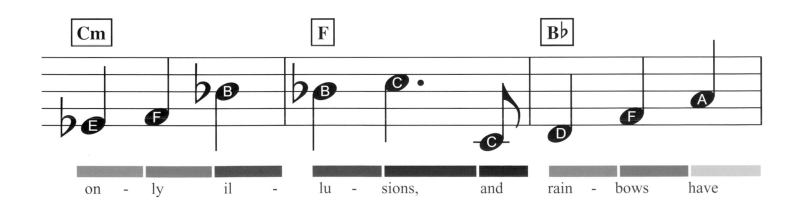

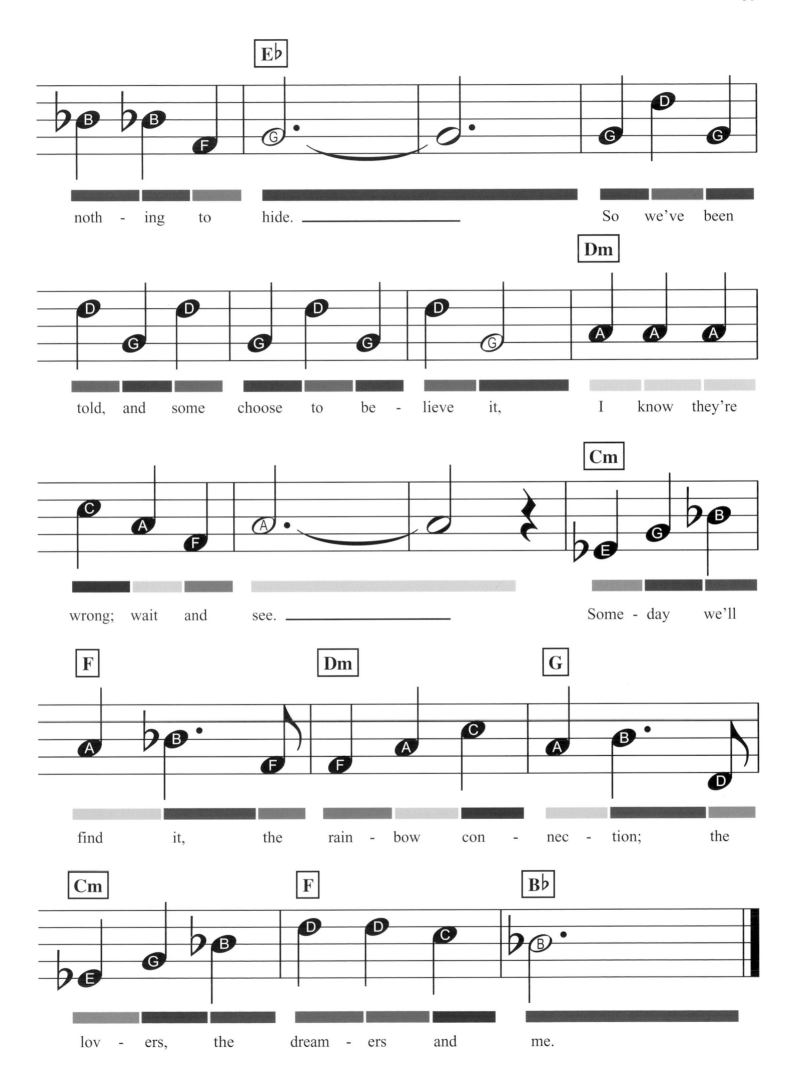

STAND BY ME

Words and Music by JERRY LEIBER,
MIKE STOLLER and BEN E. KING

Registration 8
Rhythm: Country or Rock

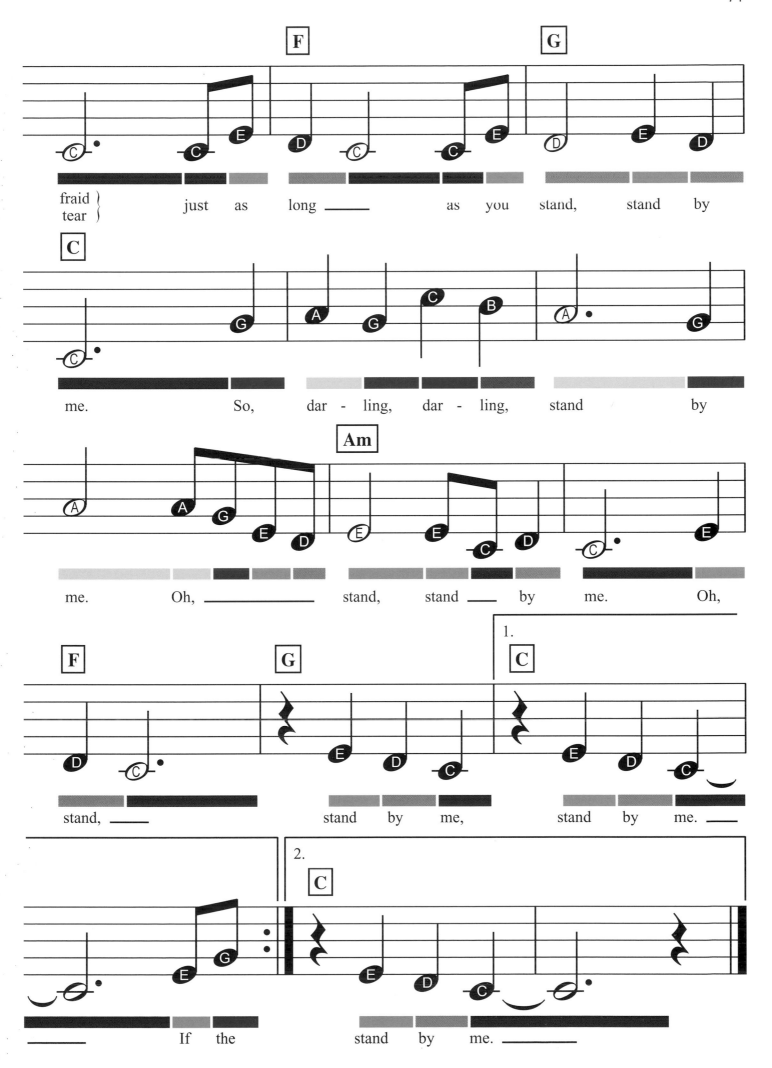

Maze Fun

Ollie the Octopus is running late! Help him to get
below the "C" in time to meet Stan the Starfish!
How many different paths can you find?

SUGAR, SUGAR

Words and Music by ANDY KIM
and JEFF BARRY

Registration 1
Rhythm: Rock

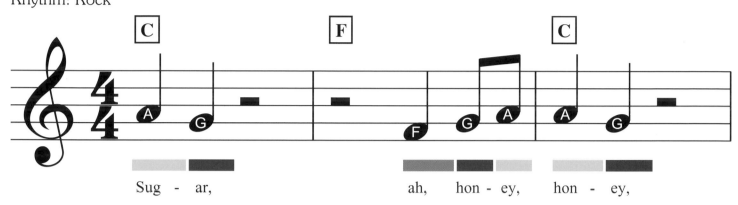

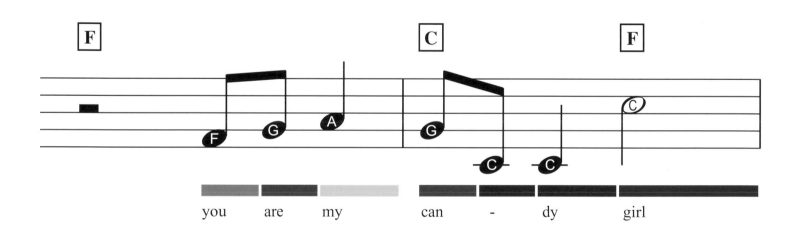

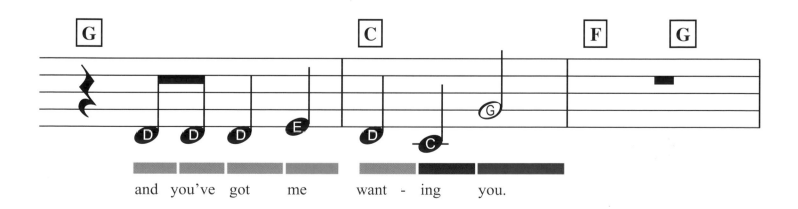

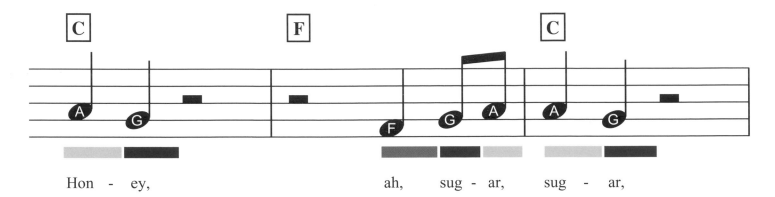

Hon - ey,   ah, sug - ar, sug - ar,

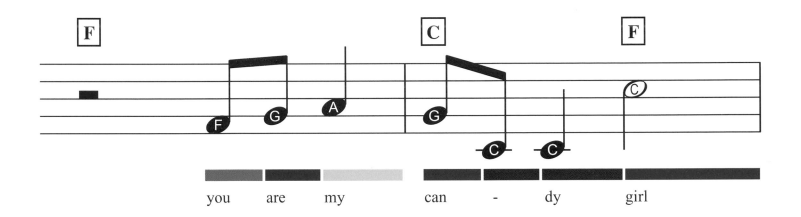

you are my can - dy girl

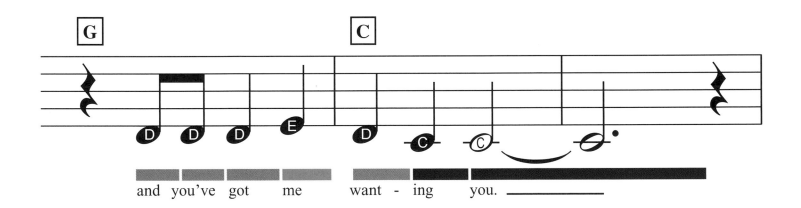

and you've got me want - ing you. _____

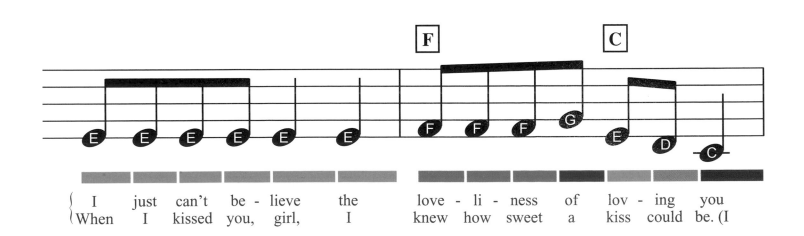

{ I just can't be - lieve the love - li - ness of lov - ing you
{ When I kissed you, girl, I knew how sweet a kiss could be. (I

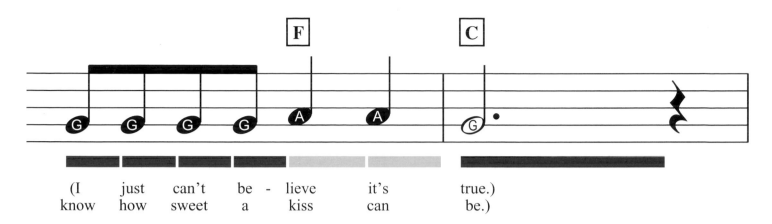

(I   just   can't   be - lieve   it's   true.)
know   how   sweet   a   kiss   can   be.)

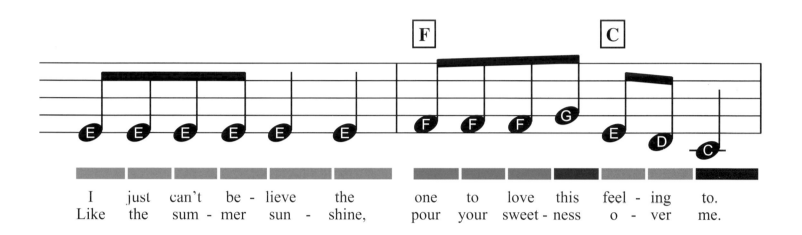

I   just   can't   be - lieve   the   one   to   love   this   feel - ing   to.
Like   the   sum - mer sun - shine,   pour   your   sweet - ness   o - ver   me.

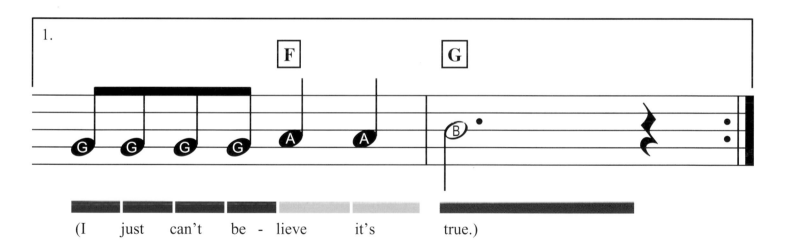

(I   just   can't   be - lieve   it's   true.)

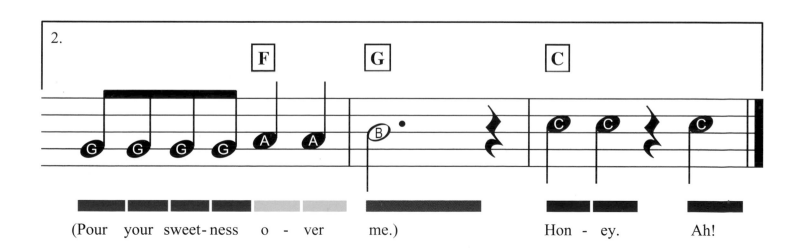

(Pour   your   sweet - ness   o - ver   me.)   Hon - ey.   Ah!

SURFIN' SAFARI

Words and Music by BRIAN WILSON
and MIKE LOVE

Registration 4
Rhythm: Rock or Swing

WINNIE THE POOH
from Walt Disney's THE MANY ADVENTURES OF WINNIE THE POOH

Words and Music by RICHARD M. SHERMAN
and ROBERT B. SHERMAN

Registration 2
Rhythm: Fox Trot or Ballad

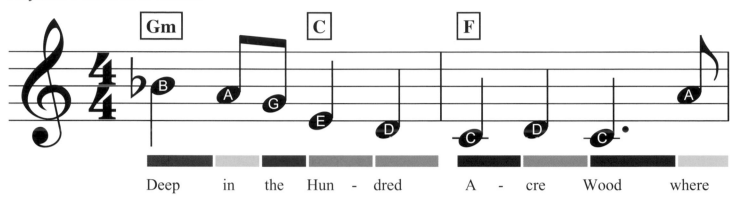

Deep in the Hun - dred A - cre Wood where

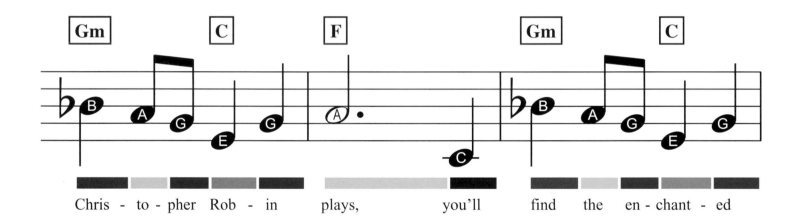

Chris - to - pher Rob - in plays, you'll find the en - chant - ed

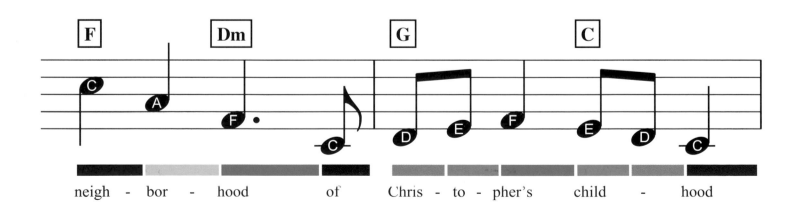

neigh - bor - hood of Chris - to - pher's child - hood

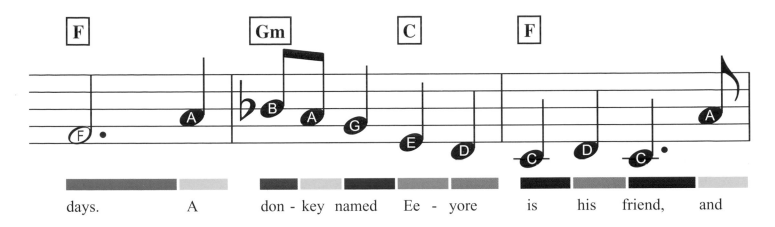

days.   A   don - key named Ee - yore   is   his   friend,   and

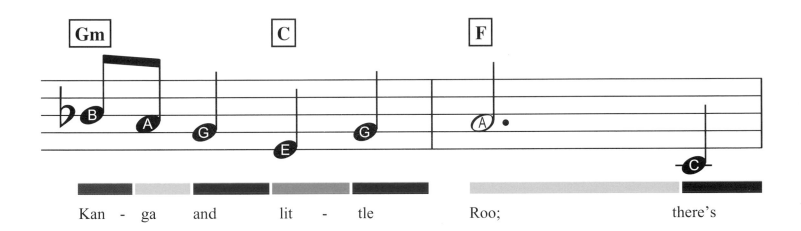

Kan - ga   and   lit - tle   Roo;   there's

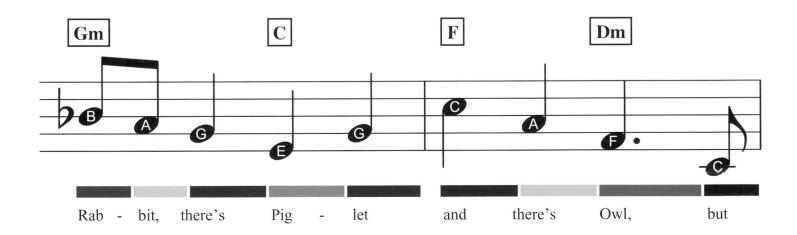

Rab - bit, there's   Pig - let   and   there's   Owl,   but

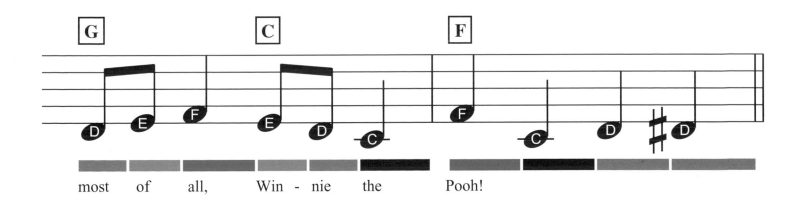

most   of   all,   Win - nie   the   Pooh!

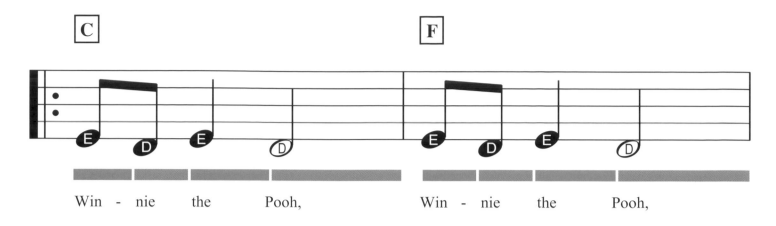

Win - nie the Pooh, Win - nie the Pooh,

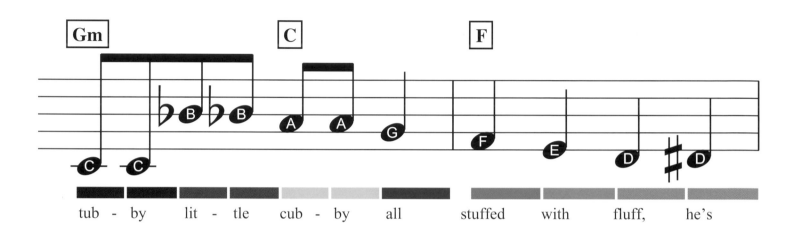

tub - by lit - tle cub - by all stuffed with fluff, he's

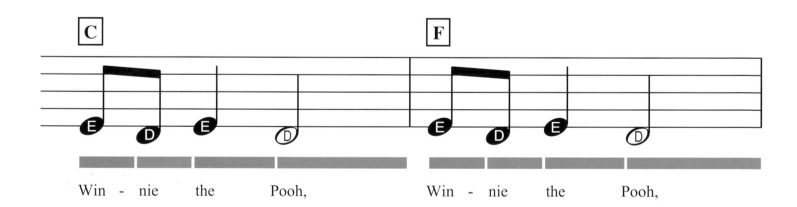

Win - nie the Pooh, Win - nie the Pooh,

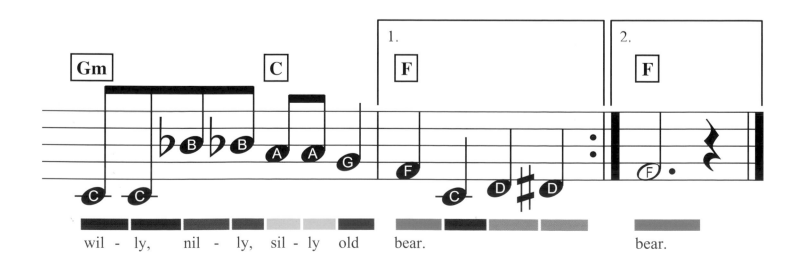

wil - ly, nil - ly, sil - ly old bear. bear.

THIS LAND IS YOUR LAND

Words and Music by
WOODY GUTHRIE

Registration 9
Rhythm: Fox Trot

82

Music Matching

This exercise is fun and will help you to identify musical signs. Just draw a line from each musical term to the picture that matches the term.

eighth note

quarter note

half note

dotted half note

whole note

quarter rest

half rest

whole rest

treble clef sign

tie

bar line

repeat sign

sharp sign

flat sign

WON'T YOU BE MY NEIGHBOR?
(It's a Beautiful Day in the Neighborhood)
from MISTER ROGERS' NEIGHBORHOOD

Words and Music by
FRED ROGERS

Registration 8
Rhythm: Swing or Shuffle

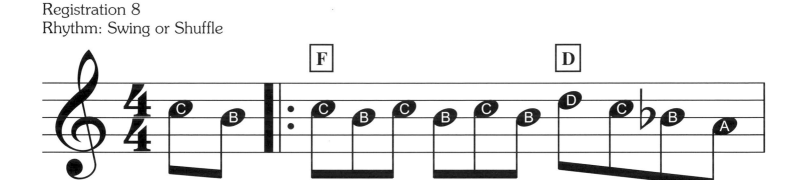

It's a beau - ti - ful day in this neigh - bor - hood, a
neigh - bor - ly day in this beau - ty wood, a

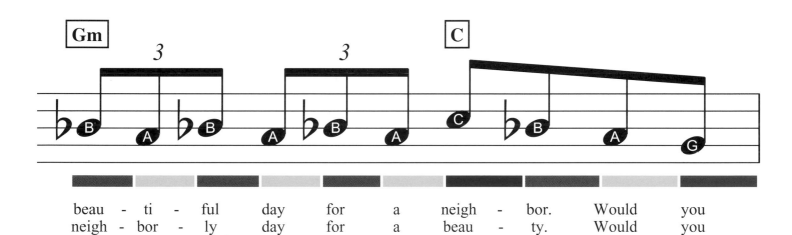

beau - ti - ful day for a neigh - bor. Would you
neigh - bor - ly day for a beau - ty. Would you

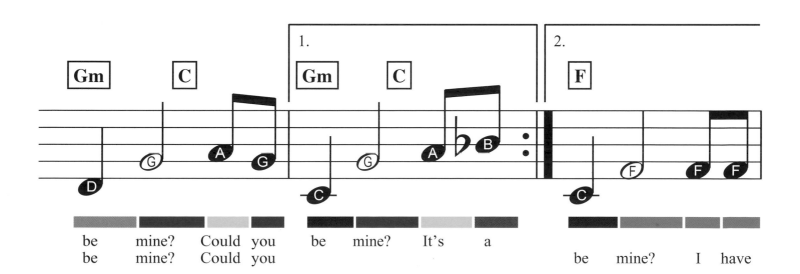

be mine? Could you be mine? It's a
be mine? Could you be mine? I have

84

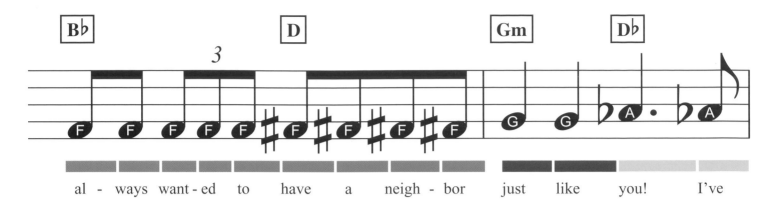

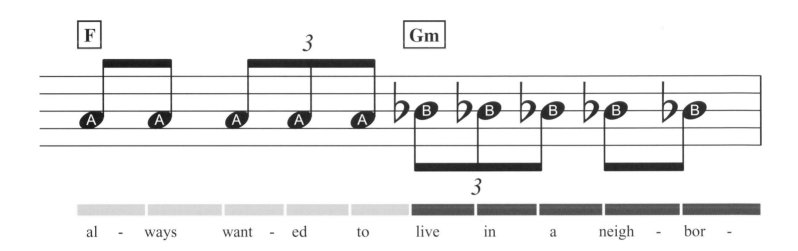

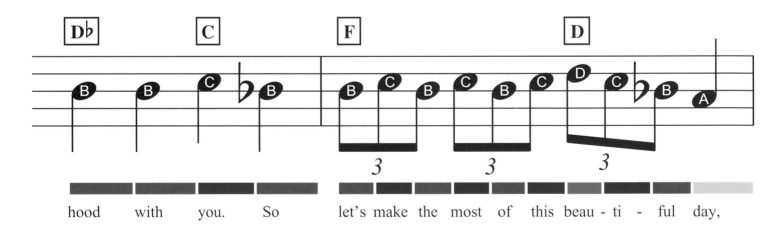

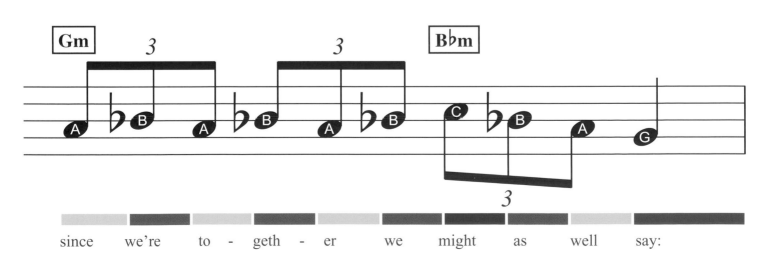

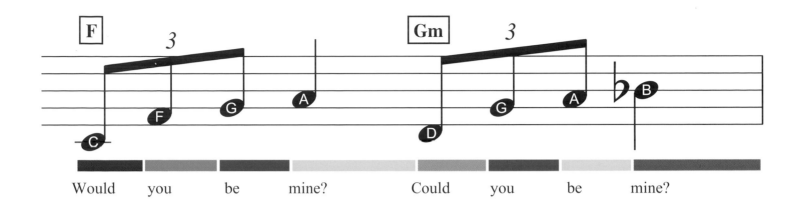

Would you be mine? Could you be mine?

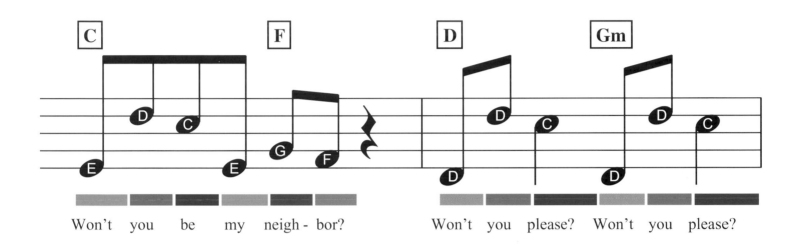

Won't you be my neigh - bor? Won't you please? Won't you please?

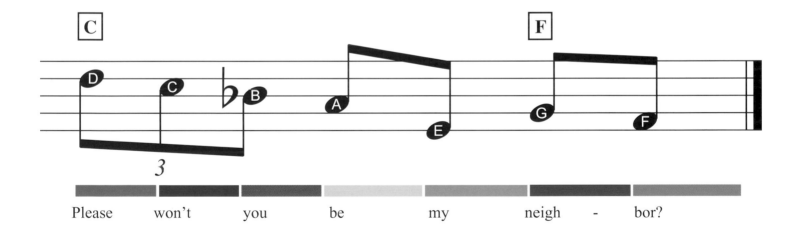

Please won't you be my neigh - bor?

YELLOW SUBMARINE

Words and Music by JOHN LENNON
and PAUL McCARTNEY

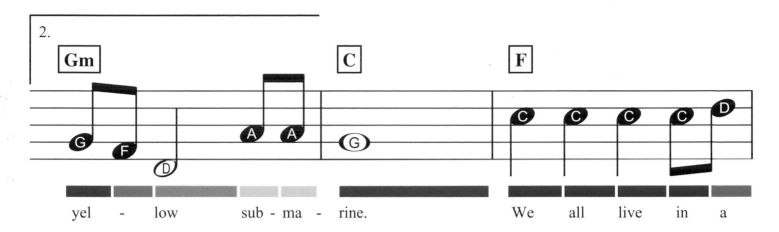

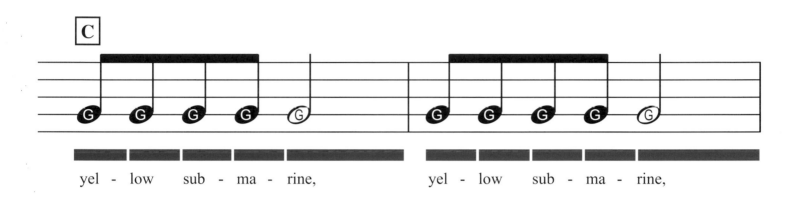

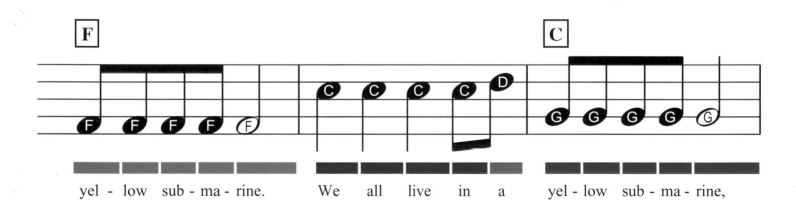

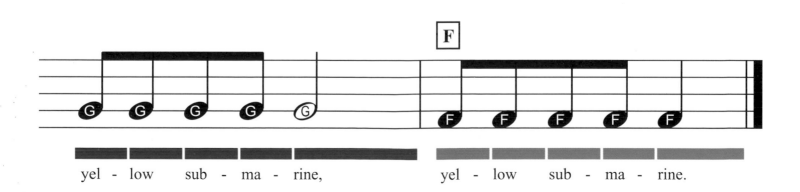

Answer Key

Pages 14-15

3 Letter Words

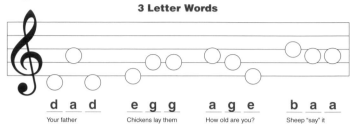

<u>d</u> <u>a</u> <u>d</u>   <u>e</u> <u>g</u> <u>g</u>   <u>a</u> <u>g</u> <u>e</u>   <u>b</u> <u>a</u> <u>a</u>

Your father   Chickens lay them   How old are you?   Sheep "say" it

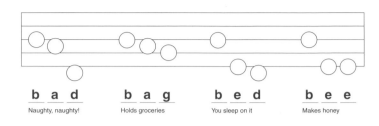

<u>b</u> <u>a</u> <u>d</u>   <u>b</u> <u>a</u> <u>g</u>   <u>b</u> <u>e</u> <u>d</u>   <u>b</u> <u>e</u> <u>e</u>

Naughty, naughty!   Holds groceries   You sleep on it   Makes honey

4 Letter Words

<u>c</u> <u>a</u> <u>g</u> <u>e</u>   <u>d</u> <u>a</u> <u>d</u> <u>a</u>   <u>b</u> <u>e</u> <u>a</u> <u>d</u>   <u>d</u> <u>e</u> <u>e</u> <u>d</u>

You keep birds in it   Baby talk   You can make necklaces from them   Do a good ____ every day

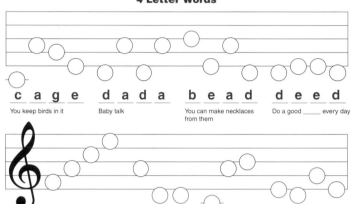

<u>f</u> <u>a</u> <u>c</u> <u>e</u>   <u>a</u> <u>d</u> <u>d</u>   <u>c</u> <u>a</u> <u>b</u>   <u>e</u> <u>d</u> <u>g</u> <u>e</u>

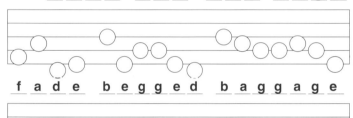

<u>f</u> <u>a</u> <u>d</u> <u>e</u>   <u>b</u> <u>e</u> <u>g</u> <u>g</u> <u>e</u> <u>d</u>   <u>b</u> <u>a</u> <u>g</u> <u>g</u> <u>a</u> <u>g</u> <u>e</u>

<u>b</u> <u>a</u> <u>b</u> <u>e</u>   <u>b</u> <u>e</u> <u>e</u> <u>f</u>   <u>c</u> <u>a</u> <u>b</u> <u>b</u> <u>a</u> <u>g</u> <u>e</u>

Page 24

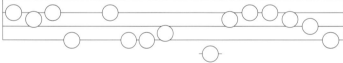

<u>f</u> <u>e</u> <u>e</u> <u>d</u>   <u>a</u> <u>d</u> <u>e</u>

Page 62

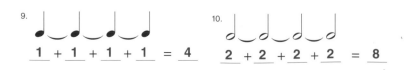

1. <u>2</u> + <u>1</u> = <u>3</u>

2. <u>1</u> + <u>1</u> + <u>1</u> = <u>3</u>

3. <u>2</u> + <u>2</u> = <u>4</u>

4. <u>4</u> + <u>1</u> + <u>2</u> = <u>7</u>

5. <u>4</u> + <u>2</u> = <u>6</u>

6. <u>1</u> + <u>4</u> = <u>5</u>

7. <u>4</u> + <u>1</u> + <u>1</u> = <u>6</u>

8. <u>4</u> + <u>4</u> = <u>8</u>

9. <u>1</u> + <u>1</u> + <u>1</u> + <u>1</u> = <u>4</u>

10. <u>2</u> + <u>2</u> + <u>2</u> + <u>2</u> = <u>8</u>

Page 82

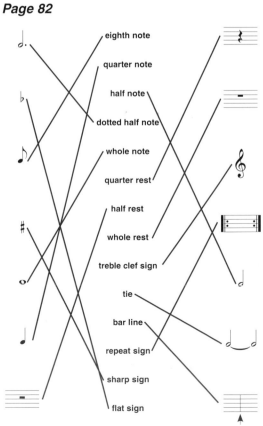

eighth note
quarter note
half note
dotted half note
whole note
quarter rest
half rest
whole rest
treble clef sign
tie
bar line
repeat sign
sharp sign
flat sign